# PLANNING FOR INFORMATION AS A CORPORATE RESOURCE

## THE BEST OF LONG RANGE PLANNING

*Series Editor*: Professor Bernard Taylor, Henley Management College

The aim of this series is to bring together in each volume the best articles on a particular topic previously published in *Long Range Planning* so that readers wishing to study a specific aspect of planning can find an authoritative and comprehensive view of the subject, conveniently in one volume.

Whereas each issue of *Long Range Planning* normally contains a 'horizontal slice' of Long Range Planning at a particular time, in different fields and in various kinds of organizations across the world, each volume in the new series will take a 'vertical slice' through more than a hundred issues, pulling out the outstanding articles on a given subject.

**Titles in the** *Best of Long Range Planning* **Series:**
**Strategic Planning — The Chief Executive and the Board (Number 1)**
Edited by Bernard Taylor

**Entrepreneurship — Creating and Managing New Ventures (Number 2)**
Edited by Bruce Lloyd

**Making Strategic Planning Work in Practice (Number 3)**
Edited by Basil Denning

**Planning for Information as a Corporate Resource (Number 4)**
Edited by Alfred Collins

Later volumes will deal with other topical themes
**Developing Strategies for Competitive Advantage (Number 5)**
Edited by Patrick McNamee

**Strategic Planning for Human Resources (Number 6)**
Edited by Sheila Rothwell

**Strategic Management of Services (Number 7)**
Edited by Denis Boyle

**Strategic Management in Multinational Companies (Number 8)**
Edited by Nigel Freedman

Each volume will contain 10–12 articles, and about 120 pages. In due course they will provide a comprehensive and authoritative reference library, covering all important aspects of Strategic Planning.

**A Related Journal**
LONG RANGE PLANNING★

The Journal of the Strategic Planning Society and of the European Planning Federation.

*Editor*: Professor Bernard Taylor, Henley — The Management College, Greenlands, Henley-on-Thames, Oxon RG9 3AU, UK.

The leading international journal in the field of long-range planning, which aims to focus the attention of senior managers, administrators, and academics on the concepts and techniques involved in the development and implementation of strategy and plans.

★Free sample copy gladly sent on request to the Publisher.

# PLANNING FOR INFORMATION AS A CORPORATE RESOURCE

Edited by

## ALFRED COLLINS

*Coopers & Lybrand Associates Ltd., London*

## PERGAMON PRESS

Member of Maxwell Macmillan Pergamon Publishing Corporation
OXFORD · NEW YORK · BEIJING · FRANKFURT
SÃO PAULO · SYDNEY · TOKYO · TORONTO

| U.K. | Pergamon Press plc, Headington Hill Hall, Oxford OX3 0BW, England |
|---|---|
| U.S.A. | Pergamon Press, Inc., Maxwell House, Fairview Park, Elmsford, New York 10523, U.S.A. |
| PEOPLE'S REPUBLIC OF CHINA | Pergamon Press, Room 4037, Qianmen Hotel, Beijing, People's Republic of China |
| FEDERAL REPUBLIC OF GERMANY | Pergamon Press GmbH, Hammerweg 6, D-6242 Kronberg, Federal Republic of Germany |
| BRAZIL | Pergamon Editora Ltda, Rua Eça de Queiros, 346, CEP 04011, Paraiso, São Paulo, Brazil |
| AUSTRALIA | Pergamon Press Australia Pty Ltd., P.O. Box 544, Potts Point, N.S.W. 2011, Australia |
| JAPAN | Pergamon Press, 5th Floor, Matsuoka Central Building, 1-7-1 Nishishinjuku, Shinjuku-ku, Tokyo 160, Japan |
| CANADA | Pergamon Press Canada Ltd., Suite No. 271, 253 College Street, Toronto, Ontario, Canada M5T 1R5 |

First edition 1990

**Library of Congress Cataloging in Publication Data**

Planning for information as a corporate resource/edited by Alfred Collins—1st ed.
    p.  cm.—(The Best of long range planning: no. 4)
1. Management—Data processing.   2. Management information systems.   3. Information technology—Management.   I. Collins, Alfred.   II. Series
HD30.2.P586  1990    658.4'038—dc20     89-26670

**British Library Cataloguing in Publication Data**

Collins, Alfred
Planning for information as a corporate resource.
1. Organisations. Management. Information systems.
Long-range planning, Business strategy
I. Title    II. Series
658.4'038
ISBN 0-08-037270-8 (Hard cover)
ISBN 0-08-037409-3 (Flexicover)

*Printed in Great Britain by BPCC Wheatons Ltd, Exeter*

# Contents

# Planning for Information as a Corporate Resource

*Alfred Collins, Coopers & Lybrand Associates Ltd., London*

## The I.T. Revolution

In the period during which the papers in this volume were published, society has experienced a profound revolution. Information technology has truly come of age. This period could well be called the formative years of the "Age of Information".

The 1960s saw the application of computer technology in *First Generation* applications. A fundamental characteristic of these applications, batch processing, changed the traditional job role of the clerical worker. The systems emulated the process of clerical activity but moved much of the repetitive processes into new centralized 'computer factories' (data centres) with their own internal, but often remote, work processes.

During the last years of the 1960s and early 1970s 'on line' computing emerged and provided the impetus for the *Second Generation* of computing. The availability of the interactive computing terminal (visual display unit or VDU) extended the scope of computers to business areas previously untouched. Airlines handled large volumes of bookings on-line, utilities introduced on-line customer services, etc.

The Second Generation of applications were still directed towards cost displacement by handling large scale, repetitive tasks but a significant amount of the job processes now extended outside the walls of the 'computer factories' and came back into the hands of the clerical staff.

During this period the mini computer developed, database technology emerged and systems complexities grew rapidly. Many of the systems were built on simple organizational lines with interfaces between them operating in 'batch mode'.

The impact of computer technology was restricted to dealing with large systems which were easily structured. This inevitably meant that data was processed but the less structured information, such as text, image and voice communications, were handled separately and with very different technologies.

The *Third Generation* of technology led to the concept of processing information in an integrated way and the era of Information Technology arose. After 1975, the speed of the revolution grew rapidly. Significant factors influencing this growth were:

☆ the development of personal computers, bringing down the cost of application more rapidly than before;

☆ the emergence of word processing and its subsequent integration with personal computing and networked systems;

☆ the development of sophisticated 'wide area networks' (WAN) and 'local area networks' (LAN) for internal networking within buildings;

☆ the significant increase in computing power per £ or $ spent on large computers;

☆ the gradual emergence of international standards for information communications;

☆ the development of Facsimile or Fax as a low cost communication system which has become almost as popular as the personal computer (pc);

☆ the availability of advanced voice communications such as Cellnet.

During the Third Generation of computer technology the advances in hardware and networking concepts have been mirrored by equivalent developments in software. These developments include:

☆ relational database systems;

1

☆ modular packaged systems for pc's;

☆ the ubiquitous spreadsheet;

☆ structured software methodologies to aid development;

☆ the Computer Aided Software Engineering (CASE) tools;

☆ Fourth Generation Languages (4GL) to increase productivity in development;

                               to name but a few . . .

Against this background management have striven to come to terms with a continually evolving technology and to apply it to their business activities both to reduce operating costs and to give them added advantages in their respective markets. To do this, the leaders have successfully dealt with three major issues:

1. using information as a strategic resource,

2. applying information technology in the strategic planning process, and

3. managing information technology for strategic impact.

It is under these three headings that I have grouped the papers in this volume.

# Information as a Strategic Resource

In today's society the majority of people have a surfeit of information thrust upon them from every side. In business there is normally an abundance of data, most frequently related to internal affairs, less frequently about competitor activities. Turning data into strategically important information requires a number of processes:

a. identifying what is strategically important;
b. filtering out the unimportant;
c. identifying the sources of important information;
d. ensuring that the right people receive the right information, and
e. safeguarding strategic information.

The four papers which comprise the first section dealing with information as a strategic resource cover these issues.

## Designing Information Systems for Strategic Decisions: Hayes and Radosevich

Robert Hayes and Raymond Radosevich of Vanderbilt University, Tennessee in this paper argue the need for a new class of information system related to strategic decision making. This is the forerunner of later papers by William King and associates which address the subject in greater detail.

The authors make the case for distinguishing between information used for operational needs and that for strategic planning. In their own words:

> We should clearly distinguish between the desirable attributes of an MIS designed to provide for the operational aspects of an organization and one designed to service the needs of strategic planners.

They emphasize the need for strategic MIS or SIS — Strategic Information Systems — to take account of innovation trends and other critical factors which might impact upon an organization. They identify five problems in developing an SIS. To quote:

> 1. Information needs are rarely defined explicitly because of a lack of formal strategic planning and control systems.
>
> 2. Existing formal communications channels are ill-suited for strategic information.
>
> 3. The timing and phasing of strategic information gathering transmission, storage and retrieval is most critical.
>
> 4. Sources of strategic information are commonly external to the organization.
>
> 5. The strategic information time horizon is often the distant future (five, ten or fifteen years from the present) rather than the past.

In this paper they consider each of the characteristics above in some detail and establish a number of criteria for designing an SIS.

## Competitive Information Systems: Rodriguez & King

William King, of the Graduate School of Business, Pittsburgh has been a regular contributor to *Long Range Planning*. In this paper he and his colleague Jaime Rodriguez, address the issues associated with Strategic Issue Competitive Information Systems (SICIS).

In many companies "competitor intelligence" has been ignored. The information available concerning competitors is often "casual, cursory and wrong" as William Sammons and his associates point out in the preface to their book "Business Competitor Intelligence" (John Wiley 1984). As he continues:

This customary indifference to the competitive position and potential of the other side may be changing slowly in some corporate circles, but today most managers in most American companies regard 'competitor intelligence' as one or more of the following:

- unethical behaviour
- illegal spying
- an invitation to antitrust litigation
- unwarranted and costly research
- a minor aspect of marketing best done in an informal, intuitive fashion.

King and Rodriguez propose three criteria for SICIS, namely:

☆ competitive data when collected and processed must be in a form which supports strategic choice;

☆ data when evaluated provides information and in the strategic context must be evaluated for some specific strategic purpose or use;

☆ the collection, analysis and dissemination of information must be integrated into the formal strategic decision making process.

They emphasize the frequency of systems which failed in this field and have correlated success and failure with adherence to the criteria given above. They point out the need to focus upon strategic issues for the business as a means of focusing the requirements for information and provide clear examples of typical strategic issues and information which might be held in a SICIS. Finally they put forward a methodology for developing a system of this type.

## Planning for Strategic Decision Support Systems: King

A second paper by William King considers the role of decision support systems as part of the strategic planning process. In this article he clarifies the differences between a "management information system (MIS)" and a "decision support system (DSS)". As he puts it:

A DSS is an interactive computer-based system that utilizes decision models, gives users easy and efficient access to a significant data base and provides various display possibilities.

The variety of DSS that is specifically designed to support top management and planners in their strategic management functions may be termed a 'strategic decision support system' (SDSS).

He provides several examples of SDSS, one in the field of SICIS, the subject of the previous paper.

SDSS are essentially elements of larger computerized systems which normally incorporate databases, data management subsystems and interactive terminals. They are not simple conceptual systems. As a consequence considerable planning, design and cost is involved in their preparation.

This paper considers the planning involved in a SDSS and provides some idea of the underlying methodology involved.

## Information for More Effective Strategic Planning: King & Cleland

This paper by William King and his associates considers how a Strategic Data Base (SDB) can be developed to help the various phases of the strategic planning process. The objective of an SDB or of a number of SDB's is to organize strategic information into a form in which it can be readily and easily used in the planning process.

As King and Cleland express it:

Strategic data bases are concise statements of the most significant strategic items related to various clientele or environments which affect the organizations' strategic choices. As such they are the mechanisms through which the current situation and future opportunities are assessed.

They propose task forces to prepare SDB's because:

In this way the organization can be assured that the evaluation does not represent one narrow point of view or only the parochial viewpoint of analysts.

They outline a mechanism for preparing the SDB's and suggest the following as key SDB's to be included:

☆ Strengths and Weaknesses SDB

☆ Business and Industry Criteria SDB

☆ Competitive SDB

☆ Environmental Opportunities and Risks SDB

☆ Management Viewpoints and Values SDB

This paper when combined with the previous papers makes a valuable contribution to the understanding of the use of information as a strategic resource. They also present a useful and constructive view of some of the problems facing companies that may wish to build systems that support strategic decision making.

Today a number of companies are actively developing executive information systems (EIS) which are intended to support the needs of top management. All too often, however, these systems emulate the management information system providing a mass of information in considerable detail. In most cases this information is internal and provides historic detail.

Relatively few systems of this type take account of external information and 'fuzzy' or imprecise intelligence. Nor do the designers assess the way top management uses information in making strategic decisions.

There is still a great deal to learn in designing systems to support strategic decision-making. The technology has advanced rapidly and provides the means to do so. However, we still have to overcome top management's "techno-phobia" — the reluctance to accept technology. We also have to understand much more the human factors involved.

The next group of papers is concerned with the application of computer technology to the planning process. This is, of course, closely related to the issue of using information as a strategic resource. The three papers which comprise this section provide a good cross section of the factors involved.

# Information Technology in the Strategic Planning Process

## Computerized Corporate Planning: Boulden

This paper, based on a survey of 55 US companies, by James Boulden, President of On-Line Decisions Inc. examines computerized corporate planning systems. A computerized corporate planning system is defined as:

the use of the computer to simulate the effect of alternative strategies on the achievement of corporate objectives.

In doing so it addresses a series of key questions:

☆ Is computerized corporate planning suitable for all firms?

☆ What are the major applications?

☆ Who decides on computerized corporate planning?

☆ What are the pay-offs?

☆ What are the major problems?

☆ Does it create organization conflict?

☆ Who uses it?

☆ Who is responsible for it?

☆ How does performance compare to expectation?

This detailed survey provides a useful background to the subject of using computers in the planning process. Since the article was written, some of the technical solutions have changed, for example, time-share bureaux would largely be replaced by low cost computing facilities in-house. Also, in many instances corporate planning systems use spreadsheets and networked pc's interfacing with databases held on corporate mainframes. However, the majority of the findings of the survey are still valid.

## Experience with Corporate Simulation Models: Naylor and Schauland

Thomas Naylor of Duke University and Horst Schauland of Social Systems Inc. argue that changes are necessary if corporate simulation models are to help management to achieve their objectives.

☆ the models used must be more user-oriented;

☆ there should be more emphasis on production models (i.e. producing plans) which are linked to simulation models;

☆ there will be an increase in use of models to optimize achievement using mathematical optimization methods;

☆ there will be an increasing emphasis on integrating functional modelling (e.g. finance and production modelling) into total corporate modelling;

☆ external factors will increasingly become significant elements in modelling (see King et al. in Part 1);

☆ corporate politics will play an important role in how simulation models are developed.

This paper addresses many of the key factors that influenced those of us who were involved in the development of corporate planning systems. In the event internal optimization methods did not generally emerge as a major influence but the other factors are as relevant today as when this paper was published.

## Corporate Planning Using Government Information Systems: Hinomoto and Reddy

Professor Hinomoto and James Reddy examine the potential for using Government data for long range planning. The paper is written in the context of the USA.

A major problem facing potential commercial users of Government data is the extent to which it is up-to-date. The authors describe a system which has by-passed this problem and provides direct on-line access to Government files.

Since this paper was published considerably more data is available on-line to organizations both from central Government statistics and from companies who provide industry statistics.

In recent years the ability to relate key information to geographic coordinates has given a greater impetus to these systems. The ability of a major food company in the US to identify from population statistics the proportion of Mexican, Hispanic and white Eurasian population by geographic locality has enabled them successfully to adapt their products to meet local tastes.

The use of broad based Government information will vary with government policy from country to country. The open-access policy of the US government is significantly in advance of most other countries.

# Managing Information Technology for Strategic Impact

The five papers which make up this section are concerned with the issues affecting the management of information technology (IT) as a resource within an organization. Information technology has become a major agent of change within many companies. In many cases, when well managed and integrated with the business, it has added significantly to the success of these companies. In other cases where it has not been managed well, and where its contribution has not been understood by management it has either been neutral in its effect or, even worse, has inhibited a company from achieving its full potential.

## *Key Issues in Managing Information*: Sizer

Richard Sizer's paper is broad and philosophical and it touches upon some key factors involved in managing the information resource within a company.

Sizer makes careful distinctions between data, information and state of knowledge. The speed and volume in communication of information (incor-porating data), assisted by computer technology, can significantly influence the decision making and state of knowledge within an organization. Data management, he suggests, is important in this context.

Organizations have applied computers both centrally and locally with varying degrees of success. The reason behind this variation in success, he believes, is due to the confusion between the distribution of information handling and the distribution of "intelligence". Those companies which have distributed processing but retained strong central policy units seem to have succeeded more often.

He also considers a major and growing concern — that of *computer fraud* and associated criminal actions using computers. The emergence of the 'hacker' has made many companies reconsider the ways in which they implement sensitive systems.

## *A Management Strategy for Information Processing*: Collins

This paper provides a useful case history of the application of a planning methodology for information technology. The system described, Business Systems Planning, is one of the most widely applied methods and is provided as a value added service by IBM to their clients.

Essentially, the method attempts to align the IT strategy with business strategy and, as a starting point, assumes that a well developed business strategy has been put in place. In practice, in many companies that is not true.

Today there are many planning methods which can be applied to align IT and business strategy. However, it should be stressed that the use of methodology is not a guarantee of success. The key factors that lead to success are:

☆ a sincere commitment to the process by top management;

☆ a study of information needs driven by business-men and not IT technical considerations;

☆ assigning the best quality team from within the company;

☆ employing compatible external consultants who both have experience and understand the business issues and the business environment of the company.

The study described in this paper was successful because these criteria were met.

## Managing the Growth of Electronic Office Information Systems: Hirschheim

In this chapter Rudolph Hirschheim, London School of Economics, considers a major problem that companies increasingly face — the rapid rate of technological change. He argues that coping with the pace of technological change will be vital for survival in the 1990s.

There are three trends which have major impacts on companies:

☆ the pace of technological change;

☆ the pace of world wide environmental change; and

☆ the growth of industrial democracy and employee participation.

He believes that electronic office systems will play an increasingly important role in helping organizations to adapt to the changing environment. He considers it essential for organizations to develop strategies for electronic office systems. He adapts Nolan's Stage Theory of Data Processing Growth to the development of Office Information Systems and he uses cases to illustrate the concepts he puts forward.

The case examples which he uses apply as effectively today as when the paper was written.

## Information Technology — Its Impact on Property Development: Burrows

The application of information technology within any organization carries with it implications for the design and development of the property used. Local area networks require new cabling with connection interfaces at frequent intervals. As the computers used grow in capacity, new specialized environments are required. The greater reliance of an organization on information technology requires the back up of power supplies, stand-by computer centres, resilient wide area networks, etc.

This chapter examines some of the implications of the wide-scale application of IT for property development. Brian Burrows argues that a number of factors have emerged:

☆ a lack of suitable premises;

☆ a shortage of people with the necessary skills; and

☆ social attitudes which resist change.

He examines the implications for industrial factory units, the concept of the Science Park and the evolution of the office. He also considers in detail the current limitations on office accommodation in terms of the design requirements for IT.

## The Realities of Electronic Data Interchange: How Much Competitive Advantage?: Benjamin, DeLong and Scott Morton

During the last eight years there has been a significant growth in computer-to-computer links between trading partners; for example, a manufacturing company may order directly from a supplier using total electronic information transfer. Such systems use technology known as "Electronic Data Interchange".

Initially companies such as American Airlines, with its SABRE system, and Thomson Holidays with its TOP system used these network links to gain competitive advantages in their markets. Most of the well quoted examples of using information technology as a competitive weapon used this principle.

There has been a considerable move in recent years to try to develop standard message formats for various areas of trading. At the international level organizations such as EDIFACT have made significant advances in achieving international acceptance of standards. At a national level organizations such as the Electronic Data Interchange Association in the UK are working to achieve harmony on a national scale.

Thus the two forces are opposed:

☆ this desire to retain a unique system with competitive advantage, and

☆ the move to harmonize systems via international standards.

The next five years will see major changes occur in the lines of battle.

This paper examines the issues and problems that confront organizations which implement EDI, describing three detailed cases. Their conclusion is that EDI is rapidly becoming an essential way of doing business rather than a means of providing a unique competitive weapon.

The authors believe that

those organizations that do succeed in gaining significant competitive advantage from EDI will do so by learning how to integrate the technology effectively into their organizations in such a way that they can continually add valuable new capabilities to the system while deriving cost savings from increased productivity and decreased overheads made possible by EDI.

This is an area which will become increasingly important in the application of IT to business over the next five to ten years. This chapter makes a useful contribution to understanding how to succeed.

# PART ONE

# Information as a Strategic Resource

# Designing Information Systems for Strategic Decisions*

**Robert L. Hayes and Raymond Radosevich**

Graduate School of Management,
Vanderbilt University, Tennessee

In this article the authors argue that recent events have given rise to a need for a new class of information related to strategic decision-making. They describe some of the characteristics of "ideal" systems to meet this need and suggest a program of less sophisticated systems which will develop towards that ideal.

ORGANIZATIONS REQUIRE VAST AMOUNTS of information to carry out their managerial functions. Historically, the task of gathering data, processing the data into information, and disseminating information has been left to functional groups to handle as they felt best. Accountants have devised systems for transforming financial data into information that indicates how well the company is doing, marketing men have devised systems for gathering product/market data and converting it into sales forecasts and new product needs, and production schedulers have developed information systems for facilitating the conversion of raw materials into inventories of finished goods delivered to warehouses throughout the nation. In addition, provision has been made for making condensed versions of these functional information flows available to top management in order that they might oversee the entire operation.

Two developments took place in recent years which have had significant impact on the way that information is treated within organizations. First, the process of information creation has come to be treated as an object of study. The gathering of data, the processing by both man and machine into usable information, the communication to the user, and the evaluation

and eventual decision making have all been studied under the single classification—management information systems. The second development concerns the increased emphasis being given by top management to long-range planning and strategic, as opposed to operational, decision making. This shift has created a need for a new class of information, and the characteristics of that information and the systems for providing it will be the subject of this discussion.

We should clearly distinguish between the desirable attributes of an MIS designed to provide for the operational aspects of an organization and one designed to service the needs of strategic planners. The operational side is concerned with the efficient exploitation of the current product-market-technology position of the firm. Vast amounts of data are created in the day-to-day functioning of the enterprise, some of it in the form of historical, accounting-type reports and others concerned with forecasts of financial, marketing, and production factors. The MIS must be designed to efficiently process this vast quantity of data into useful information for management to employ as a basis for operating decisions. All of the problems discussed in the literature on information systems — communication channels, filtering, data storage and retrieval, determination of information needs, etc.—are relevant to this design process. The problem is often summarized as getting the right information to the right people at the right time in a form they can understand and will use.

The problem facing the designer of an MIS for use by strategic decision makers could almost be stated in those same words. There are, however, subtle but vital differences in the form which the information usually takes and costs associated with missing or incomplete data. Some examples are in order here by way of clarification.

(1) In the early 1950's the young and booming electronics industry was setting sales and profits records using a technology based on the vacuum tube. Meanwhile, a few scientists in distant laboratories were busy inventing a device, the transistor, which would overnight render the vacuum tube obsolete. A few firms suffered substantial losses because they delayed preparation for transistor technology while others seemed to have kept abreast of the situation and were prepared to exploit it. In at least a few of the firms that were caught napping, the cause could be directly attributed to an MIS whose capability was limited to compiling accounting reports and processing extrapolative-type forecasts.

(2) The bank credit card phenomenon is another interesting example. In this case the innovation was highly visible to most executives in the banking industry, whether or not they were served by an adequate environmental monitoring system. Many banks, lacking a mechanism for converting such obviously important pieces of raw data into meaningful assessments of strategic relevance, jumped on the credit card bandwagon. The disastrous consequences of such actions have been well documented in recent years.

(3) Educational institutions have recently provided a near-perfect example of the ills that can beset organizations which choose to operate in isolation from their environment. Historically disdainful of planning over any but the shortest of time horizons, universities have frequently found themselves in the position of producing a product (for example, professional school graduates) which is either outmoded or in poor juxtaposition with required entry-level skills in the profession. For many years the high demand for college graduates of almost any description led to a willingness to overlook certain shortcomings in their preparation. Events of

* This article is based upon the 4th Report from Vanderbilt Institute of Strategic Management.

the past half-decade have precipitated crises, both financial and otherwise, at scores of prestigious educational institutions. Federal and state governments, quite accurately viewing the educational budget as a decisive political instrument, began to use funding cuts as a means for quelling ideological dissent. The excess demand for college graduates suddenly turned into an excess supply and potential employers could choose more carefully among applicants. Finally, many colleges heavily committed to faculties, facilities, and programs in the sciences and engineering experienced a decline in both federal research grants and student enrollment. Using extrapolative forecasts of past growth patterns as the basis for planning new programs has led many universities to the brink of financial disaster and a few beyond the brink.

In the light of these examples let us examine some of the characteristics which tend to differentiate information required for strategic decisions from that needed for operational decisions. Before we begin, we should consider the distinction between data and information. Data can be defined as the set of stimuli that impinge on the organization or are created by it. Although it is in raw, unprocessed form, it could not really be described as "random" since its collection is biased somewhat by the positioning of the organization in the environment. Information can then be thought of as the result of a transformation which casts the data into a framework appropriate to the activities of the organization. The problem of information system design can then be considered as the construction of this transformation following analysis of the likely inputs and the desired output.

A list of characteristics of information systems for strategic decisions is presented in Table 1. An explanation of these characteristics and how they differ from those of information systems for operating decisions follows.

**Table 1. Characteristics of Strategic Information Systems.**

1. *Information needs* are rarely defined explicitly because of a lack of formal strategic planning and control systems.
2. Existing formal *communication* channels are ill-suited for strategic information.
3. The *timing and phasing* of strategic information gathering, transmission, storage, and retrieval is most critical.
4. *Sources* of strategic information are commonly external to the organization.
5. The strategic information *time horizon* is often the distant future (five, ten, or fifteen years from the present) rather than the past.

*Information needs.* Programmable decisions made at the lower levels of management and in the operations area typically are based on few variables and simple relationships. Once decision models are formulated, and perhaps even automated, it is a relatively easy task to define the information needs and the consequent information systems. Recent surveys of formal procedures for strategic decisions [c.f., Ringbakk[1]] have shown that very little comprehensive planning and virtually no coordinated control or implementation takes place at the strategic level.

*Communication channels.* The vast majority of existing formal information channels are designed to process routine, internally - generated information. Informal channels process most of the information needed for strategic decisions but even these informal channels are wholly inadequate. For example, professional specialization develops language and knowledge bases which make communication difficult with managers outside of the specialty. In addition, geographic dispersion of dissimilar functional groups and a lack of understanding of the strategic management role add to the difficulty of facilitating the formation of communication.

*Timing and phasing.* The value of certain information to strategic decisions is often not perceived by the original sensor of the raw data. This problem is compounded since most information arrives out of phase with its need and requires storage and processing to be highly relevant to strategic decisions. Once stored, the unstructured information is difficult to retrieve since current coding procedures are relatively inefficient.

*Sources.* Since strategic decisions are primarily responsible for mapping the firm's activities onto its environment, the primary information source is external to the organization. Much valuable information, such as the pending invasion of a market by a new competitor, is proprietary and carefully guarded. That which is available from the public domain is often very expensive to obtain, although certain trends promise a reduction of costs (such as computer-based data from industrial trade associations or government - generated census or scientific clearinghouse data).

*Time horizon.* Most information for current management decisions is historical in nature. Accounting data and information for control are all descriptions of past or current events. The generating of strategic plans, their

implementation, and the design of means for evaluating their progress all involve horizons stretching into the distant future. The simple assumptions underlying extrapolative forecasting (as little as even this technique is used) make it inapplicable for any but the shortest time spans.

Underlying these statements are a number of assumptions about the managerial environment which should be made explicit.

(1) The present rates of change in technology and in the marketplace continue.

(2) A substantially increased share of profits will accrue to the firm which can either anticipate or manipulate change as opposed to the firm which can only react to it.

(3) The focus of top management will continue its present shift from a concentration on operational to a concentration on strategic problems.

(4) Within the foreseeable future, the inventory of tools in the management sciences which are directly relevant to transforming strategic information into strategic decisions will remain severely limited.

## SOME PRESCRIPTIVE CONSIDERATIONS

The challenge to a designer of a system for providing top management with the information it needs for strategic decision making is indeed demanding. As a basis for our discussion we shall arbitrarily divide the information generation process into data collection, communication, processing, evaluation.

The entire problem is exacerbated by most managers' lack of experience in planning and strategic decision making. In considering what steps might be taken to implement a strategic MIS, we shall assume that the organization has or is developing some kind of formal, comprehensive planning process. To accompany this process, formal systems for control and implementation will have to be designed before information needs can be specified. This formal systems must be developed in consonance with management attitudes and organizational cultures which are supportive of strategic management (Radosevich and Hayes).[2]

### Data Collection

Although, as was pointed out earlier, the source of much of the data is external to the organization, most areas of the environment are informally monitored by some organizational member as part of his routine operational activity. This is not to say that visibility necessarily implies recognition, but in many cases it does mean that the data gathering mechanism is partially in place. What needs to be added is the motivation and the skill on the part of these organizational members to perform the initial filtering and feed the output into an appropriate communication channel. Most firms already operate this way for certain kinds of decisions. New products, for example, are frequently the result of information inputs from marketing or field engineering. For strategic information requirements there is a need to formalize and expand this already existent data gathering capability. If it is to succeed, it will not be as a completely off-line activity but one which complements the operational duties of the organizational participants.

As an alternative to incorporating strategic data gathering into the operational duties of existing organization sub-units, a firm might wish to set up a new staff unit whose sole function is this single activity. Such a tactic certainly has some very important advantages. For one, the members of such a unit are not required to divide their efforts between two tasks; the reward system design problem is somewhat ameliorated. In theory, at least, members of such a unit can become better trained, more effective observers of the environment and thus able to perform their function more efficiently. It may also be possible to turn such a group to think more like strategic decision makers so that the evaluation which goes into all such data gathering is more closely directed towards organizational goals.

There are also some clear disadvantages to such an arrangement. The range of search of such a sub-unit is necessarily smaller than that of the entire organization. Representative as it might be, it could not hope to be subject to as large and as diverse a set of environmental stimuli. A second disadvantage lies in the possibility that the goals of the sub-unit may evolve in such a way as to diminish its effectiveness in performing its original mission. While it is difficult to predict just what form this evolutionary process might take, we might wish to make some general statements based on past observations of organizational behavior.

(1) Because the group may feel a need to justify its existence by producing some output, it may narrow its search to include only those areas where the implications of developments are well understood and easily agreed upon.

(2) For the same reason, the energy of the unit may be directed simply to turning out a document rather than at worrying so much about collecting data.

(3) Group members may come to see themselves as staff planners rather than

environmental monitors. Although the organization needs both, it has made provision for planning elsewhere.

A great deal has recently been written on environmental surveillance and monitoring systems but most of the applications are still in the experimental stages. Some of them are concerned primarily in expanding the field of search and the number and sensitivity of sensors to the environment.[3] Others recommend primary emphasis on developing formal systems internal to the organization first in order that guidelines are developed to select the right data and communication to the ultimate user is assured.[4] Many writers recognize the need for simultaneous development of both.[5]

## Data Communication

As was discussed earlier, designing the data transmission subsystem is a problem for a number of reasons: the data are of an unusual form (qualitative as opposed to numerical) and hence less precise and less amenable to summary; they frequently have farther to travel from source to user and hence the opportunity for filtering or noise input is enhanced; and their relationship to the current operational situation may be unclear or nonexistent. In the face of these difficulties, it would seem unwise to attempt to incorporate the communication of strategic information into pre-existing, operational channels.

We have been discussing a bottom-up form of communication—the transmission of data from the gatherers to the users. Equally important for the case where already existing organizational units are to serve as information collectors is the top-down communication of goals, guidelines, and planning and other procedures. While almost everyone would agree to the necessity of providing some basis on which search should proceed and initial evaluation be carried out, something far more significant is really called for.* Top management must do more than simply provide collection guidelines; it must relinquish its privacy with regard to the goals of the organization, exposing them to public view and hence to the possibility of public and stockholder criticism. While it is not intended that all organizational secrets should be laid bare, it is clear that search cannot be allowed to proceed randomly, and any form that direction might take must implicitly concern goals and long-range plans.

## Data Processing

A primary concern of the processing function for strategic information systems

*Ackoff asserts that one of the primary problems of management mis-information systems is an overabundance of irrelevant information.

is to add the element of futurity to the raw data which are usually historical in nature. To this end, the utilization of appropriate forecasting techniques must be an integral part of any formal strategic information system. While it is difficult to choose the appropriate technique without considerations of cost of application, processing time, length of history available, formality of the decision models, and other factors, one can generalize to some extent by using a surrogate measure for many of these factors—the stage of the life cycle of the product or service about which information is being processed. Figure 1 illustrates this point by dividing a typical life cycle into four stages — exploratory, initial growth, steady growth or constant level, and decline.

In the exploratory phase there are no sales, or at most only trial marketing experiments, and hence no histroic data base for the extrapolative, statistical forecasting routines. As a result, the predictions of experts and groups of experts are gathered, compiled, and tested for consistency through iterative processes using techniques like Delphi, scenario writing, morphological and cross-impact analyses.

In the initial growth phase, trial sales efforts are interpreted to provide long-run projections of market size and share for plant and equipment decisions. Analysis of comparable products (e.g., the last generation of computers) and other market research techniques can be used for these projections. Short-run decisions on production and inventory levels can be based on forecasts using a variety of sensitive exponential forecasting methods. The sensitivity to turning points is here crucial and again the lack of historical data that is relevant to future trends precludes most extrapolative techniques.

Once in the steady-growth or constant-level phase, operations in this product/ market have become fairly routinized and a significant data base starts to build up. Extrapolative techniques which examine the statistical properties of time series (such as trends, cycles, seasonality, and random components) can be routinely employed here. If this is a very high volume and profitable line, the cost of building econometric models may be justified. Towards the end of this phase the identification of the downward turning point is again critical. Various tracking techniques employing statistical control models can here be used to great advantage, particularly if the random component of the time series has exhibited stochastic stability.

In the decline phase, futurity can again be added to the information by employing the techniques used in the early

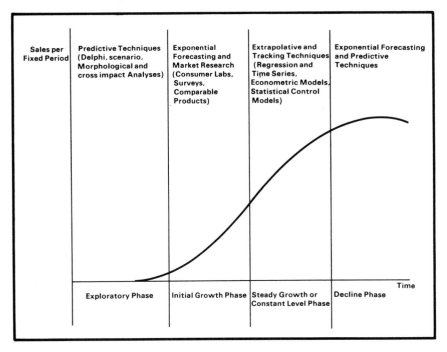

**Figure 1. Alternative Forecasting Techniques for Use in Different Stages of the Product Life Cycle.**

phases of the life cycle. Once strategic decision making has been formalized to the point of routinely introducing new ventures and divesting unpromising operations, the concepts and techniques, such as those just described, of managing a portfolio of product/market life cycles can be adopted.

In the same way that futurity can be added to information, explicit recognition of uncertainty can be incorporated in the data processing of strategic information systems. Information presented in deterministic form (a single value or "best" estimate) is considerably less valuable for strategic decisions than is information which explicitly incorporates probablistic statements of ranges or confidence intervals.

**Evaluation**

The value of information is of importance to the systems designer for two reasons: (1) cost-effectiveness issues in the design process are difficult to assess without some notion of end-product value, and (2) a well-designed information system will seek to provide the ultimate user with some assistance in making judgments about the value of the information he receives.

In an operational framework the quantitative nature of the information facilitates the employment of formal decision models. The use of Bayesian statistical procedures can sometimes be helpful in providing a measure of information value. However, most strategic decisions cannot be modeled with the detail and rigor required by these procedures and so less formal qualitative approaches must be sought.

One such approach is to examine the various characteristics of information that contribute to both its cost and its value and examine the trade-offs that can be made for a selection of cost-value combinations. For example, the timeliness of information is an important variable affecting both cost and value. Information can usually be made available at any of a wide range of time lags with cost increasing as response time becomes shorter. Although a decision maker may be unable to put a precise value on a given response time, he may be able to choose from among a number of alternatives based on internalized, subjective measures of value and some more objective cost estimates.

**CONCLUSION**

Earlier in this paper we stated that various developments in recent years have given rise to a "need" for a new class of information related to strategic decision-making. Having outlined some of the differentiating characteristics between this and operational decision-making and their effect on system design, we might conclude with a comment on the rather obvious difference between a "need" for this new type of information and a "demand" for it.

The information system is one of the major subsystems of an organization. An equally vital and far less frequently studied component of every organization is the set of management capabilities, attitudes, and objectives, especially as they relate to planning and strategic management. To the extent that these two activities have only recently been of concern to management, the development of an information system to support them should, in theory, proceed simultaneously with the development of a strategic planning system. The time scale for the effective development of consistent formal and informal systems for strategic management is in the range of five to ten years, depending upon the state of current systems. Although "ideal" systems having characteristics such as those described in this paper should be designed as an eventual target, a series of less sophisticated interim systems should be planned as part of the implementation plan of the "ideal" system. This step-wise approximation to strategic systems recognizes the general development of organizational capabilities and structures which must occur simultaneously if the formal systems are to be operated effectively.

**REFERENCES**

(1) K. A. Ringbakk, Organized Planning in Major U.S. Companies, *Long Range Planning* (December 1969), pp. 46–57.

(2) Raymond Radosevich and Robert L. Hayes, *Management Systems for Organizational Innovation*, Report No. 1, Institute for Management Innovation, Graduate School of Management, Vanderbilt University (November 1971).

(3) James R. Bright, Evaluating Signals of Technological Change, *Harvard Business Review* (January–February 1970), pp. 62–70.

(4) Francis J. Aguilar, *Scanning the Business Environment*, New York, Macmillan Co. (1967).

(5) Richard N. Foster Organize for Technology Transfer, *Harvard Business Review* (November–December 1971), pp. 110–120.

(6) Russell L. Ackoff, Management Misinformation Systems, *Management Science* (December 1967), pp. B-147–156.

# Competitive Information Systems

*Jaime I. Rodriguez and William R. King*

*The problem of keeping abreast of relevant competitive developments for strategic purposes is common to many organizations. In this article the authors describe a system which they have developed and which is currently in operation which they believe can prove beneficial in meeting this need. They believe that their system provides competitive data in a useful form. Also it ensures that information, and not data, are processed and provided for planners and managers to support their decision-making.*

The need to know about competitors is ingrained in the minds of most successful top managers. Similarly, the literature of long-range planning is replete with references to competitive information as a basic input to planning decisions.

In some companies, the role of competitive information in planning is restricted by its apparent unavailability. In companies that have made organized efforts to collect, assess and utilize competitive information, the situation is quite the reverse. In those cases, the plethora of data which are, in fact, available creates a difficult data management problem.†

In those companies that have begun to collect and use competitive data, the need is for *strategic competitive information* rather than mere competitive data. Many companies generate competitive studies and reports as informational backup for their strategic planning activities. Yet, the state of the information art, as it applies to strategy and planning, is well characterized by a plethora of *data* and a lack of critical *relevant information*.‡

## Criteria for Strategic Competitive Information Systems

Some firms that have tried to develop competitive information systems for the support of strategic decision making have encountered difficulty in assessing the relevance of the wide variety of competitive data which one might suppose to be useful in the determination of business strategy.

The strategy concept is so encompassing that almost any competitive data can be argued to be potentially 'relevant' to the support of strategic decision making.

For a strategic competitive information system to be cost-effective, it must be developed according to specified criteria which will ensure its relevance and usefulness. There are three such criteria which have been applied in a number of firms who have successfully developed such systems.

The first criterion is that *competitive data must be collected and processed in ways that render it into a form which is suitable for the support of strategic choice.* For instance, volumes of documents describing competitive technologies or stacks of competitor's annual reports are not suitable for direct use in planning, except as they may be occasionally used to answer specific questions. As far as guidance for strategic planning, raw competitive data is nearly useless.

The second criterion for strategic relevance is inherent in the difference between data and information. *Information is evaluated data.* Of particular concern in strategic planning is that *the data be evaluated for some specific strategic purpose or use.** Too often, the competitive information which is developed for the support of strategic planning has been so unfocused as to be of little use in the planning process. Illustrative of this is the competitive data base developed by a large business equipment firm. This 'system' compiled and disseminated one-paragraph 'intelligence' statements which were

---

*Both authors are at the Graduate School of Business, Pittsburgh, U.S.A.

†See: D. I. Cleland and W. R. King, 'Competitive Business Intelligence Systems, *Business Horizons,* December (1975).

‡See: R. L. Ackoff, 'Management Misinformation Systems,' *Management Science,* pp. 147–156, December (1967).

*See: W. R. King and B. Epstein, 'Assessing the Value of Information,' *Management Datamatics,* September (1976).

input to it by sales and technical personnel and stored in a computerized memory. These intelligence assessments were prepared after visits to client firms and contacts with competitive personnel. The items in the data base were retrievable only through a 'dump' of all items related to a particular competitor or a specific time period, or both. A systems audit showed that the system was not utilized to the degree that had been anticipated in the system proposal, that it was not integrated into any decision-making process, and that the lack of evaluation and assessment of items which were input into the system led to a great likelihood of erroneous conclusions being drawn by managers on the basis of the the information supplied by the system. As a result of the audit, the system was promptly deactivated.

The third criterion which determines the relevance of strategic competitive information is *the degree to which the information is collected, analysed and disseminated in a fashion that is integrated with the strategic decision-making processes of the organization.* This will most often mean that the use of information will be integrated into the firm's annual planning cycle, so that it can be used in identifiable ways to influence strategy choice. However, strategic competitive information is also important to the process of strategy implementation and control—i.e., ensuring that plans are carried out and that they are producing the desired effect.

Many companies have developed strategic competitive information 'systems' that have failed because they do not meet this criterion. Often, this is done in the framework of a 'data bank' mentality which says, 'Let's collect all of the data that we can identify concerning competitors and it will obviously be of great use to us in formulating our plans'. The result is most often a 'room full of data' that is so voluminous, unmanageable, and unedifying that it turns out to have little real value.

Many firms have shown, to their dismay, that information systems and processes which do not rate well in terms of these three criteria are probably not worth the effort which goes into them. It is the purpose of this paper to describe a strategic competitive information system that does rate well in terms of the criteria as well as in the assessments made by manager-users. In doing so, we demonstrate the feasibility of strategic competitive information systems which can produce something other than the *ad hoc* 'special studies' which are the primary elements of most companies' strategic competitive information activities.

## Strategic Issue Information Systems

The primary vehicle for developing an informations system which meets the above criteria is the *strategic issue*. A strategic issue in this context is a business issue that is competitor-related and which must be resolved as a part of the planning process. For instance, a strategic issue might be, 'What is the capability of our competitor to produce a new product in line X next year?' The

resolution of such an issue would provide a sound basis for the strategic planning of product development investments and new product introductions.

A strategic issue competitive information system (SICIS) is one that is developed and used in terms of such strategic issues. The ways in which such a system can meet the strategic competitive information criteria are best illustrated by contrasting it with the information *retrieval* systems which are so often developed in the competitive context.

A 'pure retrieval' system is one which permits the user to request any item or combination of items in the data base, so long as he knows in advance exactly *what* he wants, and so long as he understands the operation of the system sufficiently well to know *how* to request what he wants. Most strategic managerial needs for information are not so clean cut; thus, such systems seldom measure up to the critical criteria for strategic information.

A strategic issue competitive information system has a data base which is structured in terms of *strategic business issues.* This permits inquiries to be made in terms of *the use to which data are to be put, rather than in terms of the data themselves.* Thus, a manager using such a system inquires with an issue such as, 'What is the capability of Competitor X to introduce a new product in his Line Y next year?', he is presented with system responses which successively identify subclasses of data in which he may be interested. For instance, such a query might produce a systems response that would identify Competitor X's financial capability, production capability, marketing capability and technological capability as elements of the overall issue.

The user could then identify specific areas of interest, or he could indicate that he desires the 'total picture' related to his initial question. A user indication of interest in marketing capability might produce a successive system response indicating the availability of data on competitive distribution channel capacity, field sales capability, service capability, technical sales expertise and a variety of other marketing-related areas. The system would also indicate its ability to provide projections of future market growth.

Indications of interest in other areas would produce similar system responses which would, after each new user response, indicate successively-more-detailed sets of available data.

Of course, such a system is limited to strategic issues and questions which have been 'reprogrammed'. However, if the system is designed, as is the one described here, on the basis of those strategic issues which are identified by user-managers to be those that are most urgently needed in supporting their strategic choices, the system is likely to be used. Moreover, a system designed in this way meets the strategic competitive information criteria in ways that a pure retrieval system cannot.

The underlying premise for this variety of competitive information system that most users of complex information systems do not understand the details of the system, its mode of operation and the content of its data base. Thus, the system must be designed to facilitate use by managers who have little understanding of its intracacies. As Martin has said:

*'It is the hallmark of a good manager that he ask the right questions. He constantly varies his questioning in search for the answer which is of the most use to him. He is used to doing this with people, not machines. However, the way to extract high-level information from future information systems is likely to be to interrogate them at a suitable fast terminal with a variety of questions until their capability to provide the needed information is clarified.'\**

## The Operational SICIS

The authors have developed a strategic issue competitive information system (SICIS) that is currently in operation. Here we describe the system in detail. In the next section, we shall describe the methodology which was used in its development.

Table 1 shows the 22 issues—defined by manager users— which are incorporated into the SICIS. While these are

Table 1. List of the Strategic Issues

(1) What is the company's/competitor's ability to change price on product X.

(2) What resources limit the company's/competitor's ability to achieve goals.

(3) What is the company's/competitor's ability to deal with social issues.

(4) What are the company's or competitor's productivity strategies. <which elements are critical>.

(5) Company's resource audit.

(6) The company's/competitor's ability to grow or change.

(7) Economic criteria for external appraisal of corporation and competitors.

(8) Industry outlook for 2–10 year future.

(9) Company's or competitor's strength and weakness.

(10) Company's and or competitor's main strategies.

(11) What are the company's markets.

(12) Company's/competitor's competitive programs in product development.

(13) Company's/competitor's strategy for maintaining volume and premium price levels.

(14) Company's/competitor's effectiveness of resources.

(15) Company's/competitor's labor force availability.

(16) Field service position.

(17) Company's/competitor's sales standings.

(18) What is the company's/competitor's financial position.

(19) What is happening to the geographic focus of the business.

(20) Company's/competitor's flexibility.

(21) What is the company's position in the industry.

(22) Company's/competitor's facilities commitments.

*See: James Martin. *Computer Data Base Organization*, p. 190. Prentice Hall (1975).

not posed as generic issues, they do represent basic questions which might arise as a part of the planning process of any firm.

Each of these issues has been 'modelled' within the system so that each is divided into subclasses and sub-subclasses which constitute a logical information structure. For instance, Issue No. 13 (the company's relative position in the industry) is subdivided into the following categories:

(1) Products
(2) Perceived image
(3) Performance
(4) Market segments
(5) Service
(6) Degree of Dominance

Each of these subcategories is in turn divided into subcategories through four levels if necessary.

These hierarchical information structure models of issues provide the capability for refining the issue concerning which the user initially inquires. In this way the system user is given suggestions about areas of competitive data which are related to his initial inquiry. As well, the system can serve to focus the users interest toward a highly specific element of interest rather than the broad issue with which he has initially inquired.

Table 2 shows a computer printout which shows how the SICIS operates. In this instance, the system is programmed with data representing Tappan Corp. and a number of its competitors. These data are taken from a publically-available Tappan business policy case and a series of cases dealing with Tappan's competitors to avoid problems of confidentiality.*

The system user in Table 2 has begun by identifying his interest in both Tappan and General Electric. From the strategic issue list, he has then selected Issue No. 2— 'What resources limit the company's competitor's ability to achieve goals?' The system responds by identifying six categories of constraints ranging from 'financial conditions' to 'imposed constraints'.

The user may choose some or all of these categories for further elaboration. In effect, he can redefine the issue more narrowly than the one with which he initially inquired, or he can narrow it to encompass any, or all, of the six 'subissues'. In this case, the user selects the first and fourth subissues—those involving 'financial conditions' and 'marketing or distribution system' constraints.

Then, the system addresses each of these subissues in sequence. It first presents the next level of categories within the 'financial constraints' subissue. These are

*See: C. R. Christensen, D. R. Andrews and J. L. Bower. *Business Policy: Text and Cases* (3rd edn), pp. 323–431, Richard D. Irwin Inc. (1973).

Table 2. Strategic Issue Competitive Information System

ENTER CODES OF WHICH COMPETITORS TO EXAMINE
01—Tappen Co.
02—Design and Manufacturing
03—Sears Co.
04—General Electric Co.
99—All Competitors
1,4

ENTER ISSUE CODE OF DESIRED STRATEGIC ISSUE
IF NO MORE ISSUES DESIRED ENTER 00
2
    2—What resources limit the Company's/Competitor's ability to achieve goals?
      1—Financial conditions.
      2—Management constraints.
      3—Manufacturing efficiency.
      4—Marketing or distribution system.
      5—Research and development.
      6—Imposed restraints.

ENTER CODES OF DESIRED COMPONENTS IF ALL ENTER CODE 99
1,4
    1—Financial conditions.
      (1) Present loan levels.
      (2) Quantity of funds that can be financed internally.
      (3) Capital structure.

ENTER CODES OF DESIRED COMPONENTS IF ALL ENTER CODE 99
2
    2—Quantity of funds that can be financed internally.

**TAPPAN CO.**
(millions)

|  | 1970 | 1969 | 1968 | 1967 |
|---|---|---|---|---|
| Sales | 313 | 133·8 | 124·2 | 95·7 |
| Profits | 2·23 | 3·44 | 3·97 | 1·00 |
| Return on Assets | 2·8% | 4·5% | 5·3% | 1·9% |
| % Profit/Sales | 1·7% | 2·6% | 2·6% | 1·0% |
| Ten Year ROA | 5·9% | — | — | — |
| Ten Year Profit/Sale | — | 2·8% | — | — |

**GENERAL ELECTRIC CO.**
(millions)

|  | 1970 | 1969 | 1968 | 1967 |
|---|---|---|---|---|
| Sales | 8,726 | 8,448 | 8,381 | 7,741 |
| Profits | 328 | 278 | 337 | 361 |
| Return on Assets | 00.0% | 00·0% | 00·0% | 00·0% |
| Profit/Sales | 3·8% | 3·3% | 4·3% | 4·7% |
| Ten Year ROA | 17·2% | — | — | — |
| Ten Year Profit/Sales | — | 4·6% | — | — |

D—Marketing of Distribution.
    (1) Own us. Independent distribution.
    (2) Aggressive of passive market organization.

ENTER CODES OF DESIRED COMPONENTS IF ALL ENTER CODE 99
1
    (1) Own us. Independent distribution.

**TAPPAN CO.**
  Tappan counted with about 120 salesmen which sold to retailers, large builders, and independent distributors. Tappan was changing its distribution system and was setting up its own centralized and regional warehouses.
  Tappan franchised its servicing capability to private companies.

**GENERAL ELECTRIC CO.**
  GE controls its own channels of distribution as well as service outlets and has a potential advantage in surrounding Sears with coverage using the GE Brand, Hotpoint and Penncrest Brand.

ENTER CODES OF WHICH COMPETITORS TO EXAMINE
01—Tappan Co.
02—Design and Manufacturing
03—Sears Co.
04—General Electric Co.
99—All Competitors

ENTER ISSUE CODE OF DESIRED STRATEGIC ISSUE
IF NO MORE ISSUES DESIRED ENTER 00

00
    THANK YOU FOR USING SICIS TRY US AGAIN

EXIT

identified as 'present loan levels', 'quantity of funds that can be generated internally', and 'capital structure'. Again, the user may select any or all of these. In this run, he chooses the second only and is presented with tables of financial data for both Tappan and GE.

Then the second subissue which he previously chose—'marketing or distribution system' is presented to the user in terms of its two subcategories 'own versus independent distribution' and 'aggressive or passive marketing organization'. In this case, the user chooses only the former and is presented with narrative statements which depict this aspect of Tappan and GE's business activities. Since these particular statements are taken from dated publicly-available business policy cases, they are somewhat innocuous, but they do suggest the nature of the information which could be incorporated into the system.

After presenting these data, the system returns to its initial state and asks the user if he wishes to examine any additional firms or issues. In this illustration the user indicates that he has completed his use of the system.

## Methodology for Developing the SICIS

The SICIS described in Tables 1 and 2 was developed using a participative methodology which is a version of that described by King and Cleland.* The process involved the initial specification of strategic issues from the literature of business planning and policy and from a study of policy case analyses.† These sources provided an initial set of 23 strategic issues which were only partially defined. These issues were then assessed for redundancies

---

*See: W. R. King and D. I. Cleland, Manager-Analyst Teamwork in MIS, *Business Horizons*, April (1971).
†See for instance, J. Wall, What the Competition is Doing: Your Need to Know, *Harvard Business Review*, November–December (1974).

and content. Redundant issues were eliminated and those issues which were imbedded in another more complex issue were eliminated. The resultant list consisted of 22 issues which were more detailed than, and different from, the initial list of 23.

Next these 23 issues were discussed in small group sessions with the system's potential user-managers. These sessions served to refine the issues, to discard those which were not considered to be germane and to add others to the list. Twenty-two issues—somewhat different than the previous list of the same number—emerged from these group sessions.

The issues were expanded upon throughout this process in terms of their hierarchical content. Reference to the normative literature of planning and policy scored as a basis for further development of the information structures underlying each issue. As shown in the illustration of Figure 1, the set of issues, subissues, sub-subissues, and finally data elements, contained many common elements. Thus, the data base was developed in terms of a tree structure such as that shown there for two issues.

Figure 1 shows that different issues may entail the same subissues and data. For instance, a strength/weakness issue and an issue related to the competitor's ability to introduce a new product might both involve a subissue of 'R & D capability' and both might be supported by data on the competitor's R & D expenses, number of R & D personnel, etc.

## Conclusion

The Strategic Issue Competitive Information System (SICIS) which is discussed here is one which meets the criteria for useful strategic competitive information systems. The strategic issues which form the basis for both the structure and use of the system serve to integrate the system into the overall planning process of the company.

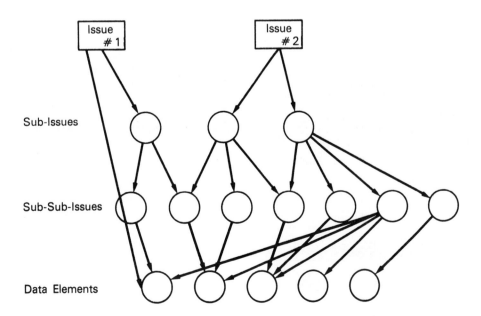

Figure 1

The SICIS does therefore render competitive data into a useful form. It also ensures that information, and not data, are processed and provided to planners and managers to support their decision making.

Such a system has capabilities which go far beyond those of typical competitive information retrieval system. As such, it can significantly enhance the effectiveness of managers in their planning roles and of organizations as they cope in an increasingly competitive environment.

---

*References*

Francois E. de Carbonnel and Roy G. Dorrance, Information Sources for Planning Decisions, *California Management Review,* **XV,** (4) 42–53, Summer (1973).

Philip S. Thomas, Environmental Analysis for Corporate Planning, *Business Horizons,* pp. 27–37, October (1974).

D. I. Cleland and W. R. King, Competitive Business Intelligence Systems, *Business Horizons,* December (1975).

Richard M. Greene, (ed.), *Business Intelligence and Espionage,* Irwin Publishing Company, Homewood, Illinois (1966).

Gathering Competitive. Information, *Chemical Engineering,* 25 April (1966).

Peter Hamilton, *Espionage and Subversion in an Industrial Society,* Hutchinson, London (1967).

Stephen Barlay, *The Secrets Business.* Thomas Y. Crowell Company, New York (1973).

Jerry L. Wall, What Competition is Doing: Your Need to Know, *Harvard Business Review,* November–December (1974).

Business Sharpens Its Spying Techniques, *Business Week,* 4 August (1975).

# Planning for Strategic Decision Support Systems

*William R. King, Graduate School of Business, University of Pittsburgh, Pittsburgh, PA 15260, U.S.A.*

*The emergence of Strategic Decision Support Systems has opened up new vistas for the true integration of formal models into the strategic planning process. However, with these new opportunities also come the need to develop planning mechanisms that will permit these sophisticated systems to achieve their potential. The process of strategic planning for Strategic Decision Support Systems that is described in this article serves to cast the organization's overall plans, strategies and strategic attributes into a framework that can be used to develop formal SDSS plans.*

In the past two decades, most large organizations have introduced and made significant use of strategic planning 'systems'.[12, 14] These systems are composed of procedures and processes for performing planning, the specification of the content and makeup of plans ('systems of plans'), and organizational arrangements for planning. They have also incorporated various 'models', such as directional policy matrices, portfolio planning models, and econometric forecasting models[4] to support the overall planning process.

However, these diverse models are often of the 'stand alone' variety that may not be well integrated into the overall strategic planning system, however supportive of strategic decision-making they may be.

A new use is being made of models in strategic management that may well serve to make them a full and continuing element of the planning process. This use is in the context of *strategic decision support systems*.

This new use of models in strategic planning systems carries with it the need for more sophisticated planning concerning their development and use. The models that have previously found widespread use in planning have been of a nature that warranted experimentation without extensive prior planning. Strategic decision support systems (SDSS) are so large, complex, expensive and demanding of the organization's resources that they must be planned for in much the same fashion as are all other such assets or activities.

## Strategic Decision Support Systems

Decision support systems (DSS) have come into prominence in the field of information systems in recent years.[7] Some use the term 'DSS' as a synonym for the currently less fashionable term 'Management Information System' (MIS). However, there are distinct characteristics that are associated with DSSs that make them unique and especially applicable to the support of strategic management.

While there are a variety of 'definitions' of decision support systems, perhaps the most practical view that may be taken of a 'true' DSS, as opposed to a MIS that has merely been renamed to give it the appearance of greater currency, is that the DSS is an integrated system that is made up of a variety of subsystems, many of the technologies for which have been in existence for some time.

The DSS is generally made up of some combination of subsystems such as:

(a) decision models;

(b) interactive computer hardware and software;

(c) a data base;

(d) a data management system;

(e) graphical and other sophisticated displays;

(f) a modeling language that is 'user friendly'.

William R. King is Professor of Business Administration at the Graduate School of Business, University of Pittsburgh, Pittsburgh, PA 15260, U.S.A.

There is no minimum set of such sub-systems that must be incorporated into a system to make it a DSS. However, most such systems involve many of these sub-systems.

Thus, a DSS is an interactive computer-based system that utilizes decision models, gives users easy and efficient access to a significant data base, and provides various display possibilities. As well, it usually incorporates a 'user friendly' modeling language, such as IFPS or SIMPLAN,[7] to give the user the opportunity to go beyond preprogrammed models to construct and use his own decision-aiding constructs. (The 'user friendly' designation is one that means that a non-specialist can readily formulate models while directly interacting with the system.)

Such systems have obvious potential for application in the strategy arena, where problems are not initially well defined, and perhaps not even well recognized or understood. The flexible capabilities of a DSS give the user (the manager or planner) the opportunity to ask for information, to test out alternative ways of viewing the problem, to subsequently ask for different information, to use preprogrammed models, to construct his own decision-aiding models, etc. Such a flexible iterative process is much like the way in which real-world strategic decision making is conducted. Many of the computerized models that have been proposed for use in planning before the DSS era,[4] were not realistic in that they presumed 'the problem' to be well-understood and well-formulated—a characteristic seldom present in strategic decision problems.

The variety of DSS that is specifically designed to support top management and planners in their strategic management functions may be termed a 'strategic decision support system' (SDSS). Whilst such systems are not in widespread use, reports on dozens of such systems have appeared in the public literature[2, 7, 16, 17] and many more are under development and consideration. For instance, Equitable Life Assurance Society has developed CAUSE, a DSS that provides computer assistance in the making of insurance underwriting decisions.[2] IBM's research division has developed GADS (Geodata Analysis and Display System) that permits great flexibility to the user in viewing spatial arrangements of data in a wide variety of situations. This system has proved to be useful in analyzing various configurations of census tracts for political redistricting, police beat design and a variety of other strategic choices that involve geographic configurations as strategic alternatives. Others, such as RCA,[17] Citibank,[17] Louisiana National Bank,[16] American Airlines,[2] and the First National Bank of Chicago[17] have reported the successful implementation of SDSSs.

## Two Illustrative SDSSs

Before addressing the topic of planning for SDSSs, it is useful to provide two somewhat-detailed illustrations.

### Strategic Issue Competitive Information System

One SDSS which has been developed and applied to the arena of competitive strategy is SICIS (Strategic Issue Competitive Information System).[14] This system has a data base that is made up of information about competitive firms in a product-market domain. The models that are an element of the system are logical hierarchical issue structures that successively decompose a broad strategic issue or strategic question, (e.g. What is our competitor's capability to introduce a new product next year?), into categories of successively greater specificity. This process allows the user to use the system and its issue models to identify relevant competitor data without requiring him to have knowledge of computer programming, the logical structure of the issue, or of the organization of the data base that he wishes to access.

An illustration of a single use of this system will illustrate these features. A user who is interested in the strategic issue, or question, dealing with competitor capabilities to introduce new products would access the system by identifying this issue and the set of competitors in which he is interested. This would elicit a system response that might identify several sub-issues—e.g. each competitor's financial, production, marketing and technological capabilities. The user would identify his level of interest in each of these and subsequently be presented with more specific sub-subissue specifications. For instance, an indication of interest in competitors' marketing capability might produce a system response indicating the availability of data on competitors' distribution channel capacity, field sales capability, service capability, technical sales expertise and a variety of other marketing-related areas. Indications of interest in other areas would produce similar system responses which would, after each new user response, indicate successively more-detailed sets of available information.

The SICIS system allows the user to peruse any or all of the sub-issues, sub-subissues, etc. that are built into the issue model. He may find that his interest is lessened once he discovers the next level of a sub-issue and he may therefore terminate his 'search' in that domain. Thus, because the system is interactive and flexible, it allows him to formulate his problem in a 'user friendly' fashion that does not require him to learn a programming language, the structure of the issue model, or the structure of a complex data base.

Perhaps most importantly, it allows the user to access a complex system in terms of his best understanding of a *problem* that he has (the issue), rather than by specifying the data or answers that he wants. Other such information 'retrieval' systems, such as those in common use in libraries, have the characteristic of requiring the user to 'know what he wants' in a very precise fashion such as in the form of keyword inquiries.[11]

### Data Resource's SDSS

Data Resources, Inc. provide a set of services, model of the U.S. economy as one element of an SDSS. Although these commercially-available services do not necessarily have all of the DSS subsystems noted earlier, they do represent an attempt to integrate a set of existing 'sub-systems' into an overall SDSS.[3]

Eckstein proposes the use of DRI's econometric model of the U.S. economy as one emelent of an SDSS that can be used for 'assumption monitoring'. This may be done by accessing various indicators such as GNP, disposable personal income, consumer prices, housing starts, etc. as is deemed relevant.

Long-term market growth may be addressed through access to long-range forecasts by market as well as to the fundamental forces that determine market growth such as demography and technology.

Costs and productivity analyses may also be conducted to provide a basis for, and assessment of, the potential of strategies involving energy savings, materials and labor productivity. These analyses may be based on access to forecasts of 'core inflation' as well as to the effects of alternative scenarios on inflation and the relative costs of plant and equipment, wages, facilities, etc. Corporate target setting may similarly be facilitated through 'peer group analysis' of competitor's financial performance data from appropriate data bases.

Business portfolio analysis may be accomplished in terms of 'bubble charts' that access models and data bases for sales and return on net assets to characterize the relative positions of business units, competitors and potential candidates for acquisition or divestiture. Such charts may be displayed using graphic display software. Acquisition candidates may be preliminarily identified in terms of specified criteria such as sales levels, profitability, and sensitivity to financial conditions.

While to this writer's knowledge, no vendor has in fact synthesized a wide range of such capabilities into a single SDSS package, they do illustrate the potential that exists for SDSS development at the other end of the 'make or buy' spectrum. SICIS, as previously described, is a SDSS that was wholly developed on an in-house basis. Eckstein's[3] illustrations of the services provided by one well-known commerical vendor illustrate how a SDSS might be developed using commercially-available products, or using a mixture of commercial products and in-house developments.

## Planning for Strategic Decision Support

Some models that have previously been used in strategic planning have been conceptual in nature, so that their development could be treated as an element of the planning process itself. The directional policy matrix[2] is an example of such a model. Others are more operational in nature, but either require moderate data support or data support that can be readily purchased externally. Portfolio models and econometric models are of these respective varieties.[4]

Little more than a cost–benefit-justified staff study or purchase decision is required to 'plan' for such models. They may be 'experimented with' with little cost or risk, adopted if they prove to be of value, or discarded if they do not.

Strategic decision support systems (SDSS) involve models that do not have these simple characteristics. Their data requirements, and the fashion in which they are used, is such that *they cannot reasonably be developed and used except as one element of a larger computerized system.* This system usually incorporates a data base, a data management subsystem, interactive computer terminals, and other DSS appurtenances.

SDSSs are of such complexity, cost and potentially have far-reaching impact on the organization and on the way in which it conducts its planning, that a more substantial planning process is required. The cost–benefit issue involves many more important intangibles, such as the likelihood that the SDSS will not be used after it has been developed at great expense, the need for users of the system to interact directly with the system rather than to use a subordinate to sit at the computer terminal and 'do the typing', the substantial requirement that 'planning data' be codified and stored in a computer memory, etc.

These intangibles, together with the cost and complexity of SDSSs, suggests that they should be planned for in much the same way as is any other highly-valued and complex organizational resource. The consequence of not doing so is suggested by the author, from a recent experience as a consultant to a company that had previously been through a series of five attempts to develop an effective SDSS, only to have all attempts fail either because the systems did not turn out to have the capabilities that were perceived to have been 'promised' when they were proposed, or they did not have 'user friendly' characteristics that made potential users willing to make use of them. The cost, in out-of-pocket terms and in terms of the time and morale of planners and system developers, was incalculable.

*Strategic Decision Support Planning Concepts*
The concept of 'strategic planning for systems' is a relatively new one. It was presented by the author in an MIS context,[10,11] was subsequently adopted by IBM,[6] and has been applied in a variety of contexts—including SDSS situations such as those described here. The concepts are not new to planners; however, their application to the domain of systems, and to SDSSs in particular, is rather new.

The basic idea of SDSS planning is shown in Figure 1 as that of translating an 'Organizational Strategy Set' into a 'SDSS Strategy Set'. The Organizational Strategy Set is made up of elements that are the outputs, or products, of organizational strategic planning—the organization's clientele analysis, its mission, its business objectives and strategies—as well as other 'strategic organizational' attributes.

The 'SDSS Strategy Set' is made up of similar elements as they relate to the strategic decision support function. They are derived from the Organizational Strategy Set. For instance, the

'SDSS Strategy Set' may involve a strategic decision support mission statement, a set of SDSS objectives and constraints, an SDSS strategy and a specified systems design-development process.

Thus, the process of planning for strategic decision support may be seen to be one of taking the *outputs* of the organization's strategic planning and using them to plan for the strategic decision support function, much as the output might be appropriately used as a basis to planning for the marketing, production, financial and other organizational functions. In combination with the use of other strategic organizational attributes in a similar fashion, this transformation of 'organizational strategy' into 'SDSS strategy' is the essence of planning for SDSS.

*An Illustration of SDSS Planning*
The concept of Figure 1 is perhaps best understood by illustration. Suppose that a firm has selected, through its organizational strategic planning process, a number of business objectives and strategies as shown in Table 1. Further, suppose that a number of strategic organizational attributes has also been identified by system planners as being potentially relevant to the various varieties of SDSS

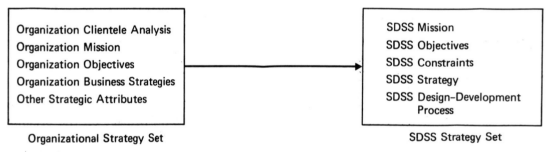

Figure 1. SDSS planning

Table 1. Illustrative Organizational Strategy Set

| Organizational objectives | Organizational strategies | Strategic organizational attributes |
|---|---|---|
| $O_1$: To increase earnings by 10% per year | $S_1$: Diversification into new businesses | $A_1$: Highly sophisticated management |
| $O_2$: To improve cash flow | $S_2$: Improvements in credit practices | $A_2$: Poor recent performance has fostered a recognition of the need for change |
| $O_3$: To maintain a high level of customer good will | $S_3$: Product redesign | $A_3$: Most managers are experienced users of computer services |
| $O_4$: To be perceived as socially responsible | $S_4$: To improve productivity | $A_4$: High degree of decentralization of management authority |
| $O_5$: To produce high quality, safe products | | $A_5$: Business is highly sensitive to the business cycle |
| $O_6$: To eliminate vulnerability to the business cycle | | |

Table 2. SDSS Strategy Set

---

**SDS mission**
    To permit the efficient and effective assessment of alternative business strategies in terms of organization's mission and objectives using the best available data to complement managerial judgment

**SDSS objectives**
    $SO_1$: To predict the potential performance of prospective new products based on historical data and the proposed characteristics of the products $(O_1 – O_6, S_3, A_2)$
    $SO_2$: To permit the effective identification and assessment of potential acquisition candidates $(O_1, O_2, O_6, S_1, A_2)$
    $SO_3$: To provide a capability for the continuous monitoring of overall performance and the degree to which organizational objectives are being achieved $(A_1, A_2, A_4)$

**SDSS constraints**
    $SC_1$: The availability of funds for SDSS development may be significantly reduced in periods of business downtruns $(A_5)$
    $SC_2$: The system must provide the capability for managers at corporate, business unit, and divisional level to obtain and *use* performance data at the relevant organizational level $(A_4, SO_3)$

**SDSS Strategies**
    Design SDSSs on modular basis $(SC_1)$. Design so that benefits may be directly derived from each module as it is completed $(SC_1)$
    Develop 'performance and objectives database' and related sub-systems initially $(SO_3, SC_1)$

---

that the organization might develop. These illustrative objectives, strategies and attributes are identified in Table 1 by appropriate subscripted letter designations.

For purposes of our limited illustration, Table 1 may be thought of as comprising the 'Organizational Strategy Set'. The 'clientele analysis' of other elements are omitted for simplicity. Greater detail on these omitted portions are discussed in King.[10]

Table 2 shows elements of an illustrative 'SDSS Strategy Set' that is derived from the Organizational Strategy Set of Table 1. As shown in Table 2, the SDSS Strategy Set consists of a broad SDS mission statement that clearly identifies what the overall SDSS function is to accomplish. The SDSS Strategy Set also entails a set of SDSS objectives. In Table 2, each of these objectives is keyed to the elements of the organizational strategy set from which it is derived. For instance, the second SDSS objective—that of identifying and assessing acquisition candidates—is directly based on three of the organization's business objectives $(O_1, O_2$ and $O_6$ from Table 1), one of its strategies $(S_1$ in Table 1), and one strategic organizational attribute $(A_2$ in Table 1).

Table 2 also shows a strategic constraint $(SC_1)$ under which development must occur. Because of a strategic attribute of the business $(A_5$ in Table 1), the availability of funds may be reduced in periods of business downturn. This, in turn, leads to an SDSS development strategy that directs that SDSSs be developed on a modular basis[8] so that if funds are cut off, benefits will be derived from those modules that are already developed.

Another related strategy is based on the same constraint, as well as on the logical primacy of the SDSS objective related to the monitoring of overall performance and of the degree to which organizational objectives are being achieved $(SO_3)$. It calls for the development of a 'performance and objectives' database as the first module of an overall SDSS.

A second constraint $(SC_2)$ is derived from the decentralized organizational attribute $(A_4)$ and the SDSS objective dealing with performance assessment. It stipulates that the SDSS must readily provide data and the ability to manipulate appropriate data in the fashion implied by a proactive planning process to managers at the corporate, business unit and divisional levels.

*References*

(1) D. F. Abell and J. S. Hammond, *Strategic Marketing Planning*, Prentice Hall (1979).

(2) Steven A. Alter, *Decision Support Systems: Current Practices and Continuing Challenges*, Addison-Wesley (1980).

(3) O. Eckstein, Decision support systems for corporate planning, *Data Resources U.S. Review*, February (1981).

(4) J. H. Grant and W. R. King, *The Logic of Strategic Planning*, Little Brown (1982).

(5) W. F. Hamilton and M. A. Moses, An optimization model for corporate financial planning, *Operations Research*, **21** (1973).

(6) IBM, *Business Systems Planning: Information Systems Planning Guide* (1981).

(7) P. G. W. Keen and M. S. Scott Morton, *Decision Support Systems: An Organizational Perspective*, Addison Wesley (1978).

(8) P. G. W. Keen and G. R. Wagner, DSS: an executive mind support system, *Datamation*, November (1979).

(9)  W. R. King, *Marketing Management Information Systems,* Van Nostrand Reinhold, Petrocelli (1977).

(10) W. R. King, Strategic planning for management information systems, *MIS Quarterly,* March (1978).

(11) W. R. King and D. I. Cleland, A new method for strategic systems planning, *Business Horizons,* **18** (4), 55–64 (1975).

(12) W. R. King and D. I. Cleland, *Strategic Planning and Policy,* Van Nostrand Reinhold (1978).

(13) F. W. Lancaster, *Information Retrieval Systems: Characteristics, Testing and Evaluation,* John Wiley (1979).

(14) P. Lorange and R. F. Vancil, *Strategic Planning Systems,* Prentice Hall (1977).

(15) J. I. Rodriguez and W. R. King, Competitive information systems, *Long Range Planning,* December (1977).

(16) Ralph H. Sprague and Ronald L. Olson, The financial planning system at Louisiana National Bank, *MIS Quarterly,* **3** (3), 35–46 (1979).

(17) Gemma M. Welsch, Successful implementation of decision support systems, pre-installation factors, service characteristics and the role of the information transfer specialist, PhD dissertation, Northwestern University (1980).

# Information for More Effective Strategic Planning

*William R. King and David I. Cleland\**

*This paper illustrates how an entity—called a 'strategic data base' (SDB)—can be developed to provide important information in a form which makes it directly useful in various phases of a strategic planning process. The strategic data bases are concise statements of the organizational and environmental situations which define the organization's most salient problems, opportunities, and constraints. These SDBs may be developed through a participative process involving tasks forces which are made up of managers representing the diverse interests of the organization.*

*The strategic data bases thereby become important informational inputs to planning which can directly serve to enhance the quality of planning decisions. Moreover, the process of developing SDBs can be an important learning device for those middle managers who can become involved in such a process at a much earlier point in their career than that at which they might normally engage substantively in the organization's overall strategic choice process.*

Nearly every textbook on strategic, or long-range, planning describes the strategic planning process in terms of strategic information as well as planning activities. For instance, the simple strategic planning process of Figure 1 shows a variety of informational inputs to the 'choice' activities which comprise the process. Among these informational inputs are assessments of the organization's strengths and weaknesses, competitive information, and environmental opportunities and risks—all of which are referred to in the figure as 'strategic data bases.'

Despite the general agreement which exists in the literature and among planning professionals concerning the need for such informational inputs to strategic planning, we have found that the information which is implicitly defined in Figure 1 is often either:

not explicitly gathered and evaluated, or
gathered, but not made a substantive part of the strategic choice process.

Thus, while all planners, and most managers, appear to pay lip service to the idea that these informational input are critical parts of the overall strategic planning process, there is little evidence that they actually play such a role.

The authors can, for instance, point to a company which employed two staff people for 6 months to develop a 'competitive data base' which was to be used in the planning process. When their efforts reached fruition, they had created a room full of carefully cross-filed documents which were made no use of in planning because the data was 'too voluminous' and 'too difficult to use'. Subsequent evaluation of these competitive data resulted in the production of a very thick loose-leaf book which was put to little use for the same reasons.

In this paper, we seek to illustrate an entity—referred to as a 'strategic data base' (SDB)—which can be developed in a form which makes it useful for directly supporting the strategic planning process. In doing so, we also describe the process through which strategic data bases are developed. These strategic data base development processes thereby become intrinsic parts of the overall planning process.

The specific SDBs and processes described here are largely taken from actual experience with business firms, although the illustrations are disguised and simplified for security and expositional purposes.

## Developing Strategic Data Bases

Strategic data bases are concise statements of the *most significant* strategic items related to various clientele/or environments which affect the organization's strategic choices. As such, they are the mechanisms through which the current situation and future opportunities are assessed. The strategic data bases shown in Figure 1 reflect the influence of various forces—the environment, competitors, top management, the 'business' in which the organization operates, as well as the organization itself—on the strategic options which are available.

---

*Both authors are at the University of Pittsburgh, U.S.A.

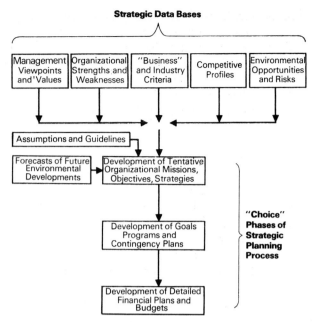

Figure 1. Strategic data bases. (This diagram, in part, utilizes ideas which are explained in *Corporate Strategy: A Synthesizing Concept for General Management* by John H. Grant. This is an unpublished research paper at the Graduate School of Business, University of Pittsburgh, 1975

These strategic data bases are essential to developing meaningful answers to the first basic question which must be asked in any planning process. 'Where are we?' Such a basic question is often reacted to by managers with one of two extreme positions—either the question is regarded to be a foolish one since, 'we obviously know where we are', or it is regarded as being adequately answered only by collecting voluminous data on all of the many aspects of the organization's status.

The approach adopted here is a middle ground between these extremes which emphasize the development of strategic data bases—*objective collections of data which are manageable, and therefore useful, in the planning process.* These 'strategic data bases' represent the *major conclusions regarding the environment and the organization's clientele*; these conclusions having been evaluated to be the *most* important such informational inputs to be considered in the planning process.

The evaluations of the vast quantities of data which form the raw input for the development of strategic data bases should be performed by task forces, or teams of managers representing diverse interests within the organization. *In this way, the organization can be assured that the evaluation does not represent one narrow point of view, or only the parochial viewpoint of analysts.*

These teams of managers, supported by staff, may be charged with arriving at *conclusions* concerning a *specified number* (usually from 10 to 15) of the *most important* factors affecting the future of the organization in a specified area. The development of conclusions on the 10–15 most important organizational strengths and weaknesses can be, as any experienced manager knows,

a difficult task, when it involves managers representing various organizational interests and points of view. *Developing a 20-page list of strengths and weaknesses could be accomplished relatively easily, but a list of the 10–15 most significant ones involves analysis and negotiation.* This is so both because of the judgments which are involved and the potential organizational impact which such a list can have through the strategic choice process.

It is useful to contrast this participative process for developing strategic inputs to the planning process with the one more commonly used to prepare the informational inputs to planning. This common approach relies on staff analysts, who gather data and prepare documents which are to serve as background information supporting planning activities and choices. Because the planners and analysts who perform these tasks often have neither the managerial expertise nor the authority to make the significant choices which are involved in any information evaluation process, the typical output of such an exercise is a document which seems to have been prepared on the basis of 'not leaving anything out'.

Such an emphasis on ensuring that nothing relevant is omitted rather than on attempting to distinguish the most relevant information from the mass of less relevant and the irrelevant serves only to perpetuate the existing state of affairs regarding the informational support provided to managers at all levels: the manager is deluged with irrelevant information, while at the same time, he is unable to find elements of information which are crucial to his function.*

Conversely, the proposed process focuses on charging task forces, which are made up of managers representing various of the parochial interests within the organization, with gathering and evaluating the data in each of a number of areas and *choosing*—through the consensual process that guides most task force decision making— those that are the most important to the development of the organization's strategy.

Thus, the 'strategic data bases' represent 'information' rather than 'data' in the sense that large quantities of data have been evaluated and condensed to a form which can feasibly be used in the strategic planning process. Thus, with the SDB approach, there is a greater likelihood that some of the information which is so universally regarded as being important to strategic planning will actually become an integral part of the strategic planning process.

Moreover, a secondary benefit which is invariably realized from the SDB approach must not be overlooked. The participative process of developing SDBs will usually involve a variety of middle-level managers from each of the organization's functional units. The SDB development process is thereby a way of involving middle managers in the 'strategic thinking' of the total organization long before they might normally become so involved by virtue of their operational job responsibilities. Thus, the SDB approach serves as a *training ground for the development of those elusive 'strategic thinking' abilities* which are so necessary to successful top-level management.

Since the best way to elaborate on the SDB concept is through illustration, we shall provide a detailed description of those data bases described in Figure 1. While these strategic data bases are somewhat generic, they also represent those with which we have worked in our consulting activities. Thus, others will most surely prove to be useful in other organizations and situations.

## Strength and Weakness Strategic Data Base

A 'strength and weakness strategic data base' is a candid and concise statement of the most significant strengths and weaknesses of the organization. While most planners would agree in principle that such a 'data base' should importantly guide strategic choice, there is little evidence to suggest that many organizations have explicitly developed strength-weakness data bases or made effective use of them. For instance, a major U.S. electrical manufacturer who got into public housing and then land development businesses might have been deterred from doing so if the organization's weakness in the basic skills necessary for success in that area had been explicitly enumerated for all to see.

Table 1 shows a strength-weakness strategic data base for one business unit of a major conglomerate. This summary list was displayed on the first page of a 'strength and weakness' planning guidebook which was prepared for use in the planning process. The remainder of the book contained exhibits which explained and elaborated on these conclusions.

Some of the items in Table 1 might be thought of as simply items describing the status of the firm, or as problems that need to be corrected, rather than weaknesses. However, in the firm's detailed explanations of these areas in their planning guidebook, they were treated as weaknesses that must guide strategic decisions, rather than merely as problems to be overcome. For instance, the details relevant to the 'low market share'

---

*See R. L. Ackoff, Management Misinformation Systems, *Management Science*, pp. B147–B156, December (1967), for a full exposition of this situation.

weakness emphasized the strategies which were precluded as a result of low market share rather than emphasizing low market share merely as a deficiency to be corrected. In this way, attention was directed toward the *strategic implications of each strength and weakness* rather than to the familiar sort of exhortations for the firm to 'do better by increasing market share'.

Two of the entries in the Strength–Weakness Table refer to the firm's 'image'. These indicate that the firm believes that its customers perceive it positively in terms of its technical superiority and (perhaps) negatively in terms of the relatively high price of its products. Such 'image assessments' are commonly incorporated into statements of corporate objectives as well as into strength–weakness analyses. Yet often, as in this instance, the firm is to some degree uncertain of just how it is perceived. In this instance, the company was not certain if its high technical quality was perceived as justifying its relatively higher price.

Such a resolution of the image situation in a state of partial uncertainty is a common, and valuable, kind of outcome of strategic data base development efforts. It points up the need for information that is more detailed and specific than that which the firm currently possesses. This result can lead to an *ad hoc* study or to the development of a more detailed information system that will provide the firm with the answers that it wants and the understandings that it needs to do effective strategic planning.

The key difference between 'strategic data bases' and the more detailed data bases which are important to information systems can now be made quite clear in the context of this illustration. 'Data bases' such as that of Table 1 require significantly more *evaluation* in their preparation than do the data bases which are commonly a part of computerized information systems.

Table 1 is the result of an evaluative process which has begun with the compilation of a long list of potential strengths and weaknesses and proceeded, through the efforts of a task force composed of upper-middle managers from all functional units of the firm, to evaluate those strengths and weaknesses which are most crucial in the determination of the firm's strategy. This concise list can then be referred to in the later phases of the planning process to suggest strategies, to aid in identifying relatively good and poor strategies, and to guide the development of plans for implementing the chosen strategies.

Table 1. Illustrative strength and weakness data base.

| Major strengths | Major Weaknesses |
| --- | --- |
| Technical expertise in centrifugal area | Low market share |
| International sales force | Lack of product standardization |
| Heavy machining capability | Poor manufacturing non-fragmented product line |
| Business systems | Poor labor relations |
| Puerto Rico facilities | Weak domestic distribution network |
| Technically superior image among customers | High price image (?) |

## Business and Industry Criteria Strategic Data Base

One informational input to planning which is widely recognized to be important, but rarely made into an explicit element of the planning process, is the key element of *what it takes to be successful in this business*. There are critical elements of 'business sense' in any activity, and while successful top executives may have a good feel for these elements, a rational planning process will make the elements explicit and available to all planning participants. Such planning inputs help to guide the choices which are made just as do the strength and weakness analyses.

For instance, the 'business criteria' which one might specify as being the keys to success in the military weapons system industry could be:

A strong research and development capability;
A commitment to using project management systems;
A strong field marketing effort closely tied in with customer organizations;
An ability to deal effectively with a relatively few knowledgeable customers;
An ability to identify and track emerging technological and market opportunities over long periods leading to consummation of sales;
Willingness to commit substantial company resources to study and prepare bids on government proposals.

In a consumer-oriented industry the requirements for success might include such factors as:

Standardization of product line components;
High volume production runs;
Highly dispersed marketing and service centers;
Low technology;
Development of a recognized brand name.

The 'Business and Industry Criteria' SDB may be developed by a team in much the same fashion as discussed previously. Their work will probably involve more interviewing of top executives and less formal data gathering than will the work of the developers of the strength–weakness data base, but ultimately, data will have to be developed to substantiate, if possible, the beliefs of top executives about the factors that are critical to success.

The format used by one company to present all of their 'data bases' is appropriate here as well—a one-page summary of the data base along with substantiating details in the form of a booklet.

## Competitive Strategic Data Base

Competition is the most apparent, and probably least understood, element of the organizational environment. In developing a competitive SDB, the organization must take care to avoid the inherent problems associated with the belief of some individuals that nothing useful

can actually be discovered concerning competitors, the reality of the voluminous material which can actually be obtained concerning competitors, and the ethical considerations which quickly come to the surface.

We have dealt with these issues elsewhere.* Here, we can merely indicate the broad insights concerning competition which can be used as guidance for the planning process in the form of a strategic data base.

For instance, competitors who are identified to be outperforming the organization can be identified and their significant actions and strategies can be cataloged and analyzed. Several major issues must be addressed with regard to competition:

First—who are the several most threatening competitors?
Second—what are the strengths and weaknesses of the competition?
Third—what is believed to be the strategy (and associated risks) of the competition?
Fourth—what resources (financial, plant and equipment, managerial know-how, marketing resources, and technical abilities) are at the competition's disposal to implement his strategies?
Fifth—do any of these factors give the competition a distinctly favorable position?

The evaluation of competition is, in a sense, a mirror image of the strengths and weaknesses of the organization itself. The competitor's ability to conceive and to design has to be evaluated. This evaluation should concentrate on his products and their design, as well as on his ability to innovate in the creation, production, and marketing of his products. Evaluation of a competitor's resources must be done in a fashion which emphasizes what each can be expected to accomplish rather than solely on the resources that are available.

## Environmental Opportunities and Risks Strategic Data Base

A wide variety of other-than-competitive environmental information can provide valuable inputs to the strategic choice process. Every organization has environmental opportunities and risks related to customers, government agencies and other 'regulators' of the organization. Profiles of some important organizational clientele can be maintained and culled of their saliencies to provide input to planning in a fashion similar to that done for competitors. This idea is particularly valuable in the case of major customers, who may be viewed in much the same way as a competitor for analytic and informational purposes.

Often, environmental risks and opportunities may be reduced to a series of specific questions, and hopefully,

---

*David I. Cleland and William R. King, Competitive Business Intelligence Systems, *Business Horizons*, December (1975).

answers which can guide planning. Amara and Lipinski* have illustrated such questions as:

Will there be widespread nationalization of industry?
What is the possibility of the development of large industry/government cartels in the United States, particularly with respect to foreign markets?
What dominant changes are likely to take place in the attitudes of the labor force—both supervisory and nonsupervisory?
Is consumerism a fad? And, if not, what directions is it likely to take in the next decade?
In what ways may the activities of multinational corporations be subject to increasing regulation?

Illustrative answers to such questions are also provided by Amara and Lipinski in a concise form which is adaptable for use in guiding the planning process:†

. . . Rail transport (both freight and passenger) is likely to be fully nationalized by 1985; all other industries (including energy-related) will remain in private hands. Financial services (insurance, banking, securities) and consumer goods industries will undergo the greatest regulatory changes.

. . . Any major shift toward industry/government cooperative arrangements (as in Japan) is highly unlikely in the near future.

. . . Workplace discontent will intensify considerably. Much of this will be due to the entrance into the labor force of the baby bulge of the late 1950s and the peculiar set of problems associated with this age group. Work incentives in the future will emphasize greater freedom of choice regarding surroundings, dress, and a decision-making role in forming teams and structuring work functions. This change involves democratization to some degree, but not of business decisions. A reversal of economic prosperity will markedly reduce the importance of psychological rewards to employees.

. . . Consumerism is not a fad. The scope of consumer protection measures will widen in the next few years; mandatory product performance guarantees are quite possible, and regulation requiring industry-wide common performance indicators and detailed reporting of product testing results is very likely.

. . . The rate of growth of multinational corporations will slow somewhat in the next decade, and multinational corporations can anticipate more international controls, both from regional codes and from global organizations. However, it is unlikely that capital controls will be bothersome to multinational corporations.

The environmental data base can, as well, entail a section dealing with general areas of opportunity which are perceived to emanate from the environment. For instance, in a business related to recreation, the increasing availability of leisure time, which can be projected from a temporal analysis of union contract provisions regarding the length of the work-week and vacation durations, might well be identified as a basic environmental opportunity for consideration.

The risks associated with these 'opportunities' should be delineated so that they are not viewed with the proverbial rose-colored glasses or treated as established facts

subsequently in the planning process. For instance, increased vacation durations among blue-collar workers might translate into increased sales of paints and other home repair items long before it affects sales of vacation homes.

## Management Viewpoints and Values Strategic Data Base

It is well understood that top management's viewpoints and values play an important role in guiding the organization. While this is completely proper, it is often not explicitly spelled out in the organization's strategic choice process. This is not to say that a 'management viewpoints and values' guidebook be provided in the same fashion as might be done for strengths and weaknesses, environmental opportunities and risks and business criteria, and the other SDBs, but it is also important that the organization not be misled into considering alternatives that have little chance to be viewed positively by top management. Participative strategic planning is a time-consuming activity and clearly, the effort should be focused in directions satisfying the practical constraints, which reflect top management views, as well as more formal resource and legal constraints. If these constraints become apparent only *after* the planning process has been conducted, it will have been wasteful and the negative effect on managerial morale will be severe. There are few more disheartening situations for a manager than to feel that he is involved in high-level decisions regarding the future of the organization only to discover that recommendations on which he has spent considerable time and effort have been rejected because they violate constraints that he was not told about.

Ackoff* has used the term 'stylistic objectives and constraints' to describe this sort of qualitative statement about what the organization will do and what it will not do. He illustrates stylistic constraints as (paraphrased):

(1) The company is not interested in any government-regulated business.
(2) The businesses into which we may go must permit entry with modest initial investments but eventually permit large investments to be made.
(3) The technology of any new businesses should be directly related to that used in current businesses.

However, the idea of 'management values and viewpoints' clearly is broader than that which is implied by these examples. For instance, it includes the *social responsibility* viewpoint of top management. Do they feel that the organization should pursue a broad multifaceted social purpose, or do they believe that the broad social good is best served if each institution seeks only a narrow range of objectives which best suits its expertise? If, in the case of a business firm, top management believes that profit-seeking does create the greatest

---

*Roy Amara and Andrew Lipinski, Strategic Planning: Penetrating the Corporate Business, p. 3, Institute for the Future, Paper P-30, November (1974).
†Ibid., p. 4.

*R. L. Ackoff, A Concept of Corporate Planning, pp. 28–29, John Wiley (1970).

social benefit that the firm itself can feasibly produce,* this belief must be translated into operational terms to guide the strategic planning process.

The general aggressive versus the defensive posture of the organization is another guide to the planning process which can only be specified by top management. If the posture is to be defensive, much time can be wasted in considering aggressive strategies which will ultimately be 'shot down' by top management review. If the general posture is stated in advance, it serves to make the planning process more efficient and more productive.

Some top executives might be reluctant to spell out their personal ideas in such a way that they will formally constrain the planning process. Their fear in doing so reflects an unwillingness to appear to be making the organization into their personal image. However, most managers recognize the appropriateness of having the

---

*See P. F. Drucker, *The Age of Discontinuity*, Harper & Row (1968), and the writings of many conservative economists, such as Milton Friedman, for the rationale for this viewpoint.

personal philosophy of top management play a role in guiding the organization's direction. Indeed, most experienced managers realize that chief executives often have as a major personal objective the making of *a distinctive personal impact* on the organization. Therefore, if the 'rules of the game' are made clear in advance, few managers will object or be disheartened; if they are not, difficulties are almost certain to ensue.

If strategic planning were solely the function of top management, this would not be a problem; but such is not the case. Therefore, a 'management viewpoints and values' SDB can play an important role in initiating a participative strategic planning process. For instance, its essence can be conveyed in a memo or letter from the chief executive which serves as a cover letter for the planning guidelines which are promulgated to initiate the planning process. Such a cover can treat, in some detail, those constraints and emphases which are to play a major role in the strategic decisions which are to be made. In this fashion, a happy medium may be struck between the extremes of burying such guidelines in the minds of top managers and requiring that they be spelled out in the formal terms that are suggested for the other strategic data bases.

# PART TWO

# Information Technology in the Strategic Planning Process

# Computerized Corporate Planning

**James B. Boulden**

President, On-Line Decisions, Inc.*

*Computerized Corporate Planning as defined in this study is: the use of the computer to simulate the effect of alternative strategies on achievement of corporate objectives; the capability of answering 'What if?' questions.*

*The increasing complexity of business firms operating in a rapidly changing environment has led many managers in recent years to consider the development of computerized corporate planning systems. This article is concerned with an in depth study of some 55 such installations in North America and Europe. The objective of this effort conducted during the period of June –November 1970, was to determine the state of the art, identify problems of installation, and project trends in the rapidly evolving use of computers in planning. Specific questions include:*

*What is the economic justification for these systems?*
*How are they being used?*
*Who is using them?*
*Have results measured up to expectations?*
*What are the costs?*
*Are organizational problems incurred?*

THE STUDY DESCRIBED IN THIS ARTICLE was undertaken for the commercial purpose of defining performance specifications for the further development of computerized planning systems and may therefore be prejudiced by the orientation of company staff. This bias is particularly noted on the emphasis placed on interactive time-shared systems rather than batch-run installations. As an auxiliary benefit, however, the study is pragmatic

*With a comment by Professor Stafford Beer, Manchester Business School, University of Manchester.

rather than theoretical. The geographic coverage includes the United States, the United Kingdom, France, Scandinavia and Canada. The industrial distribution is shown in Figure 1.

**Figure 1. Industrial Distribution.**

| Industry | Firms |
|---|---|
| Agricultural | 2 |
| Consumer Products | 4 |
| Financial | 8 |
| Foods | 5 |
| Forest Products | 9 |
| General Manufacturing | 10 |
| Pharmaceutical, Oils & Chemicals | 7 |
| Railroads & Shipping | 2 |
| Retail Chains | 3 |
| Public Utilities | 3 |
| Steel | 2 |
| | 55 |

The corporate model represents the operations and accounting practices of a company in terms of simple algebraic equations which can be run on a computer, such as Net Income = Revenue — Expense (Figure 2.)

**Figure 2. Logic for Brand I.**

| Line No. | Description |
|---|---|
| L1 | $V(I)*P(20+I)$ |
| L2 | $V(I)*P(40+I)$ |
| L3 | $V(I)*P(60+I)$ |
| L4 | $V(I)*P(80+I)$ |
| L5 | $V(I)*P(100+I)$ |
| L6 | $V(I)*P(120+I)$ |
| L7 | $L2+L3+L4+L5+L6$ |
| L8 | $L1-L7$ |
| L9 | $P(140+I)$ |
| L10 | $P(160+I)$ |
| L11 | $P(180+I)$ |
| L12 | $L8-L9-L10-L11$ |

## WHAT IS THE STATE OF THE ART?

A rather well defined evolution in computerized corporate planning has been identified trending from the complex sophisticated linear programming models of a decade ago to the modular simulation systems being developed today. The early optimizing models developed by operations research groups have been largely discarded (with the notable exception of the oil companies) because (1) policy decisions proved too complex to define in optimizing terms; (2) the organization was continually changing so that the models were no longer appropriate; and (3) operating managers could not understand the models. Unfortunately, modelling in Europe is controlled by the operations research groups and still oriented towards optimization, the search for the one best answer.

The next stage in the evolution was the development by finance and corporate planning groups of simple 'report generators' to perform the clerical labour of calculating pro forma statements (Figure 3). Concurrently, the operations research groups pursued the development of simple, fragmented models for special decision making applications, such as pricing, plant location, etc. Both of these groups have started to build interactive 'conversational' capability into the models as time-shared computer facilities have become available (Figure 4).

The latest stage in the evolution is a cooperative effort by the finance, planning and operations research groups to develop integrated modular corporate simulation systems composed of simple elements representing various parts of the organization which can be considered in isolation or in total (Figure 5). These systems work in the interactive environment with such basic decision tools as backward iteration and parameter sensitivity. Ironically, it seems these new corporate simulation systems are becoming increasingly complex so that they may suffer a similar fate to the earlier optimizing systems as reality and understanding are sacrificed for sophistication.

35

**Figure 3. Model Output Shows Projected 12-month Production and Cost of Cold-rolled Steel.**

```
                *** YEAR 70 ***      P/L FOR MODEL A
                                                                    Slabbing
   LINE ITEMS       JAN        FEB        MAR        APR
   COST/RAW MAT     8250·3     7301·2     8536·7     8986·1
   SCRAP CREDIT     −154·7     −136·9     −160·1     −168·5
   PROCESS COST     685·8      606·9      709·6      747·0
   LABOR COST       298·7      264·3      309·1      325·3
   TOTAL COST       9080·1     8035·5     9395·4     9889·9
   TIME             0·5        0·4        0·5        0·5
   TONNAGE          195·9      173·4      202·7      213·4


                *** YEAR 70 ***      P/L FOR MODEL A
                                                                    Pickling
   LINE ITEMS       JAN        FEB        MAR        APR
   COST/RAW MAT     10298·8    9114·0     10656·3    11217·2
   SCRAP CREDIT     −133·2     −117·9     −137·9     −145·1
   PROCESS COST     326·4      288·9      337·8      355·6
   LABOR COST       440·7      390·0      456·0      480·0
   TOTAL COST       10932·7    9675·0     11312·3    11907·6
   TIME             3·3        2·9        3·4        3·6
   TONNAGE          163·2      144·4      168·9      177·8


                *** YEAR 70 ***      P/L FOR MODEL A
                                                                    Finishing
   LINE ITEMS       JAN        FEB        MAR        APR
   COST/RAW MAT     11842·1    10479·7    12253·2    12898·1
   SCRAP CREDIT     −1142·6    −1011·1    −1182·2    −1244·4
   PROCESS COST     440·7      390·0      456·0      480·0
   LABOR COST       979·3      866·7      1013·3     1066·7
   TOTAL COST       12119·6    10725·3    12540·3    13200·3
   TIME             2·4        2·2        2·5        2·7
   TONNAGE          146·9      130·0      152·0      160·0
```

**Figure 4. System Orientation.**

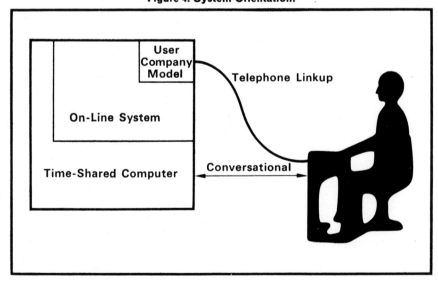

## WHY DO FIRMS COMPUTERIZE THE CORPORATE PLANNING PROCESS?

Traditional methods are too time consuming so that it is not possible to explore a number of alternatives or rapidly revise projections as conditions change. Without the computer and a corporate modelling system, it is not possible to consider the inter-relationships between the various elements of the organization and their interaction with the environment (Figure 6).

**Figure 6. What If?**

| | |
|---|---|
| ? | Raise sale price |
| ? | Increase production output |
| ? | Decrease inventory |
| ? | Labour rate up £0·2/hr |
| ? | Build new plant for £4m. |
| ? | Corporate bond issue |
| ? | Changes in reserve requirements |
| ? | Changes in earning assets |

## IS COMPUTERIZED CORPORATE PLANNING SUITABLE FOR ALL FIRMS?

A number of firms have investigated the concept of computerized corporate planning and rejected it for good reasons, primarily cost. Corporate modelling is expensive and the cost does not increase proportionately to the size of the firm. Firms such as retail organizations have rather simple corporate planning requirements which can often be handled by traditional methods. Their major concern is with the development of effective control systems. Job shops are difficult to model, although the payoff can be handsome if the installation is successful. Leadership in computerized planning goes to firms having a well defined flow of work such as steel, paper, foods, etc. A major prerequisite for installing a system, is good organization and progressive management. Otherwise, modelling may generate more problems than it solves.

## WHAT ARE THE MAJOR APPLICATIONS?

All major computerized planning installations are financially oriented with heavy emphasis on application to the preparation of annual budgets. The primary objective in this application is to shorten the time for budget development by simulating alternative strategies at the corporate level before preparing detailed budgets at the division or plant level, thus reducing the number of iterations to one. For the first time, many firms have several complete sets of alternative budgets to allow for major contingencies, and these are revised frequently as conditions change. The capability to defer making critical price/volume/ cost assumptions until the last minute is listed as a major advantage.

Surprisingly, many firms have not yet integrated their long and short range planning, and the computerized system is being used to accomplish this purpose.

Profit planning is a major application with cash planning a close second. Most firms do not seem concerned with balance sheet analysis with the exception of the financial institutions which tend to work from capital resources to derive profit estimates.

total cost of the planning system in a single negotiation for a large tract of timber. Quantitative testimonies are the exception rather than the rule. The value of corporate simulation can best be evaluated through inference since all of the correspondents reported plan to expand their systems.

**Figure 5. Idealized Information Flow.**

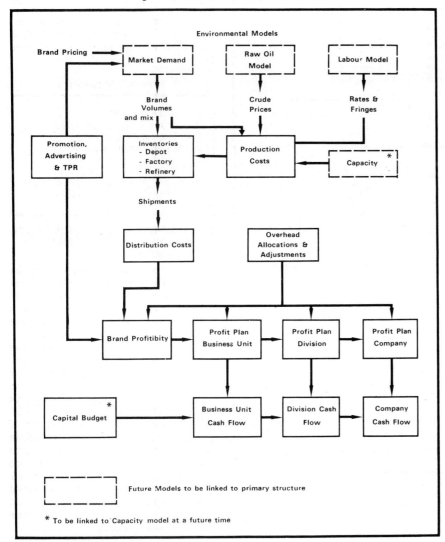

### WHAT IS THE DIFFERENCE BETWEEN REPORT GENERATION AND CORPORATE MODELLING?

The economic justification for installing a computerized report generator is that it saves in clerical labour, whereas the objective of corporate modelling is improved decision making. A very large need exists for report generators since financial statements, product profitability calculations, estimating and similar tasks consume vast amounts of clerical labour doing repetitive calculations. This use is expanding rapidly and provides an excellent first step into corporate modelling.

Corporate simulation systems include all the capabilities of the report generator plus the characteristics in Figure 7.

### WHAT IS THE PAY OFF?

As mentioned above, the objective is improved decision making, certainly a difficult goal to measure. The President of a leasing company stated he has developed an intimate feeling for his organization by personally manipulating the models (and incidently has reduced his line of credit by one third through better cash planning). A producer of lumber products states they have recovered the

### WHO MAKES THE DECISION TO INSTALL COMPUTERIZED CORPORATE PLANNING?

The answer is almost universally the chief executive and the Board of Directors. This level of sponsorship seems necessary to assure the success of the system. Further, so many firms have been disappointed in their computer investments that any decision regarding new areas of computer application must be cleared by the Board. Directors of data processing have seldom been involved in these decisions with active sponsorship normally coming from the planning and finance departments. Operations research groups have generally been an obstacle to the installation since they are oriented to more sophisticated techniques and resent the intrusion of planning and finance into their territories.

### WHAT ARE THE MAJOR PROBLEMS OF INSTALLATION?

The major obstacles are human. The traditional obstacles to organizational change such as ignorance, organizational conflict, resistance to change are all encountered with a vengance. The attitude of operating managers is typically to dare the model builder to come up with anything useful and to withhold information just to make certain he doesn't. Tradition-oriented managers fight the introduction of this new tool which invades their privacy and challenges their divinely inspired ability to make decisions.

### ARE ORGANIZATIONAL CONFLICTS CREATED?

Very definitely, especially between the long range planning department and budgeting. In almost all instances, budgeting gets custody of the system simply because it finances the development of the system. Unfortunately, the system is often used simply as a 'number cruncher' to produce budgeting reports and strategic decision making applications are ignored. The fact that the computerized planning system is a power tool used extensively by the Board and crossing sacred lines of departmentalization means that bitter battles develop over its control and application. Extensive conflicts are created between corporate headquarters and operating divisions concerned with the centralization of control.

**Figure 7. Characteristics of Computerized Corporate Planning Systems.**

1. *Selective input/output:* The user specifies the results desired in a format customized to his requirements. (Direct conversational capability is highly desirable.)

2. *Data analysis and manipulation:* Capability for data storage, retrieval, transformation and analysis.

3. *Decision Search:* Both forward and backward simulation capability to determine inputs required to achieve specified outputs at various stages in the process and levels in the organization and to compute sensitivity of outputs to inputs.

4. *Universatility and integration:* Capability of simulating all areas of the organization and linking numerous interrelated planning units as necessary to investigate transfer pricing problems, materials flow, etc.

5. *Complexity:* Capacity to handle a wide range of interrelationships between variables to simulate not only finance but total resource utilization.

## WHO USES THE SYSTEMS?

The vision of a corporate executive seated at his decision terminal is purely mythological. In only two instances were the presidents of companies actually found to personally manipulate the computer terminal and ask questions. A large number of executives have, however, trained their secretaries in operating the terminal for them and this seems to work quite satisfactorily. The normal operator is, however, an assistant treasurer or corporate consultant of equivalent rank, 30 years old, holding advanced academic degrees and having some familiarity with programming. The prevalence of a large MBA resource base has been an important factor in the growth of modelling in the United States. Aside from the two British systems which are used annually, all of the subject installations are interrogated monthly or weekly. Generally the larger firms have four to five terminals located in various functional areas and with at least one immediately available to the chief executive and the Board who are frequent consumers of its services.

## WHO IS RESPONSIBLE FOR THE SYSTEM?

Modelling (developing the symbolic relationships) is normally done by the systems group under the general guidance of a steering committee composed of representatives from various interest groups. In some instances these groups reach a completely unmanageable size, the largest on record being 23. Once the system is completed, it is almost universally placed under the supervision of the director of budgeting (in the United States). Accounting is responsible for supplying and updating the data base. Centralized control of any permanent changes in the system and the updates is vested in one full time individual in larger companies, although the system may be used by diverse groups in the firm.

## HOW OFTEN ARE THE SYSTEMS USED?

The frequency of usage is quite high during the first 6 months as the company passes through the stages of model building, test and varification. Usage may then fall as much as 50 per cent as the novelty wears off and the backlog of problems is depleted. Usage then begins to build slowly and steadily after the first year as additional applications are discovered and new users trained. Average monthly usage at the end of 1 year is approximately 50 hr of computer terminal time for a large firm and around 15 hr per month for smaller firms, although the experience varies widely (Figure 8).

## HOW ACCURATE ARE THE SYSTEMS?

The most accurate system observed was that of a large hotel which reported a maximum of only ¼ per cent variance of actual from simulated. The general performance seems to be within 1 per cent on costs with a maximum error of 2 per cent. A major advantage of these systems as compared to standard costing is that they are quite accurate outside the normal range of operations. Surprisingly however, most users are not so much concerned with absolute accuracy as with the ability to compute *relative* differences in profitability between alternative strategies. The general procedure for validation is to omit last year's data in developing the system and to subsequently simulate that period noting deviations. Many of the firms continue to operate manual systems for a period following the installation of the computer system as a check on output. Unfortunately, some operating managers expected the systems to mechanically forecast the future and in this they have been generally disappointed. The output of the computer is, of course, no better than the assumptions with which it is supplied.

## HOW DOES PERFORMANCE COMPARE TO EXPECTATIONS?

Conflicting and poorly defined expectations have constituted a major obstacle to successful utilization of the computer in corporate planning. In retrospect, most of the correspondents to the study expressed the wish that more time had been spent in the beginning developing the performance specifications to the system (Figure 9). The policy level perspective so important to the corporate planner may be a complete disappointment to the chief accountant who expects to use the system to prepare detailed departmental budgets. Most significantly, however, every company investigated was pleased with their

**Figure 8. Usage Intensity.**

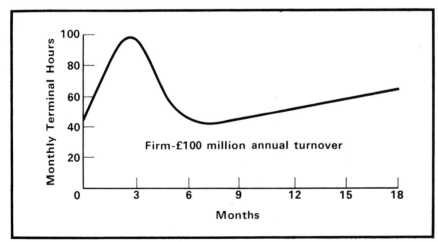

Firm-£100 million annual turnover

system at least to the extent that additional effort was being invested to extend the system throughout the organization. This is the ultimate testimony.

**Figure 9. Performance Specifications.**

1. *Cost justification:* Specific areas of application and anticipated benefits.

2. 'What If' question capabilities.

3. Time and cost schedules for accomplishing the project.

4. Who will use the system? Develop and maintain it?

5. *Modelling architecture:* Various models and their inter-relationships.

6. Definition of input–output relationships, including flow charts.

7. Identification of data requirements and availability.

8. Personnel availability for systems development, implementation, and maintenance.

## WHAT SYSTEMS CAPABILITIES ARE REQUIRED?

The most frequently mentioned feature is the capability for backward iteration—the ability to search backward from an objective or an output to determine the necessary inputs or conditions for their achievement (Figure 10). This is extremely difficult to do by hand calculation in a situation of any complexity because of the extensive interdependencies. Although discounted cash flow, risk analysis, and other financial tools are theoretically desirable, they are in fact seldom used by the firms in this study. The capability to do sensitivity analysis is, however, a basic prerequisite of an acceptable system since most users wish to investigate the importance of varying alternative assumptions as they effect profits (Figure 11). Reliability and error-free operation are essential as is the need for flexibility to conveniently make changes in the logic, output formats, and to add additional modules. Linking capabilities between models are essential.

## WHAT IS THE TIME AND COST FOR SYSTEMS DEVELOPMENT?

In-house systems groups are naturally attracted to the task of developing an interactive corporate simulation system, as it constitutes a major funding opportunity and a definite intellectual challenge. Unfortunately, the firms who have tried such developments have found the time and cost requirements much greater than

**Figure 10. Profit Iteration.**

**Metric Tons Sales of a Specific Product (Parameter 21)**
**Required to achieve a desired profit before indirect expenses (Line 15)**

| Par 21 | Line 15 in '71 |
|---|---|
| 269·7000 | 408·60 |
| 8250·7342 | 48294·81 |
| 2284·9333 | 12500·00 |

**Figure 11. Model Shows Projected Cost of Tandem Mill When Yield is Varied from 83 to 87 per cent.**

PARAMETER SENSITIVITY
PAR/MIN/MAX/INCREMENT/= 94/0·83/0·87/0·01/
*** YEAR 70 ***      P/L FOR MODEL A

PAR✻94 =        0·830

| LINE ITEMS COST/RAW MAT | JAN 9298·9 | FEB 8229·1 | MAR 9621·8 | APR 10128·2 |
| LINE ITEMS COST/RAW MAT | MAY 10064·9 | JUN 9875·0 | JUL 4057·6 | AUG 5950·3 |
| LINE ITEMS COST/RAW MAT | SEP 6203·5 | OCT 6393·4 | NOV 6646·6 | DEC 6646·6 |

PAR✻94 =        0·840

| LINE ITEMS COST/RAW MAT | JAN 9188·2 | FEB 8131·2 | MAR 9507·2 | APR 10007·6 |
| LINE ITEMS COST/RAW MAT | MAY 9945·0 | JUN 9757·4 | JUL 4009·3 | AUG 5879·5 |
| LINE ITEMS COST/RAW MAT | SEP 6129·7 | OCT 6317·3 | NOV 6567·5 | DEC 6567·5 |

PAR✻94 =        0·850

| LINE ITEMS COST/RAW MAT | JAN 9080·1 | FEB 8035·5 | MAR 9395·4 | APR 9889·9 |
| LINE ITEMS COST/RAW MAT | MAY 9828·0 | JUN 9642·6 | JUL 3962·1 | AUG 5810·3 |
| LINE ITEMS COST/RAW MAT | SEP 6057·5 | OCT 6243·0 | NOV 6490·2 | DEC 6490·2 |

PAR✻94 =        0·860

| LINE ITEMS COST/RAW MAT | JAN 8974·5 | FEB 7942·1 | MAR 9286·1 | APR 9774·9 |
| LINE ITEMS COST/RAW MAT | MAY 9713·8 | JUN 9530·5 | JUL 3916·1 | AUG 5742·7 |
| LINE ITEMS COST/RAW MAT | SEP 5987·1 | OCT 6170·4 | NOV 6414·8 | DEC 6414·8 |

PAR✻94 =        0·870

| LINE ITEMS COST/RAW MAT | JAN 8871·4 | FEB 7850·8 | MAR 9179·4 | APR 9662·5 |
| LINE ITEMS COST/RAW MAT | MAY 9602·1 | JUN 9420·9 | JUL 3871·0 | AUG 5676·7 |
| LINE ITEMS COST/RAW MAT | SEP 5918·3 | OCT 6099·5 | NOV 6341·0 | DEC 6341·0 |

anticipated. A major U.S. bank recently developed a batch run report generator but cancelled the subsequent interactive time-sharing adaptation after concluding the cost would be 10 times the original development. One of the world's 10 largest corporations recently completed an extensive technical evaluation to conclude that they could not expect a basic interactive capability for less than £150,000 ($360,000) and that this could not be justified solely for their own use. This compares with an estimated £400,000 spent in the past 3 years by a major U.S. railroad in an extensive systems development. Because of this large investment, the few organizations which have developed such systems are licensing them to other organizations as a means of recovering their investments.

## WHAT IS THE TIME AND COST FOR INSTALLING THE SYSTEM?

Somwhere between 3 days and 1 year. A large farming cooperative did, in fact, install their system in a few days due to its simplicity and the existence of well defined relationships. A more realistic estimate is 4 calendar months and 20 man-months for a sizeable company to develop the logic relationships and bring up a preliminary system. An additional 6 months by one man in cooperation with line management is necessary to tune the model to a useful state. (This assumes a large organization with relatively homogeneous operations.) A sizeable installation will, then, require approximately £20,000 and the better part of a year to install, exclusive of systems design and programming as discussed previously. The requirements will be half that for a firm of say £10 m. turnover. In most instances part of the modelling expertise is purchased outside from management consultants or similar professionals (Figure 12).

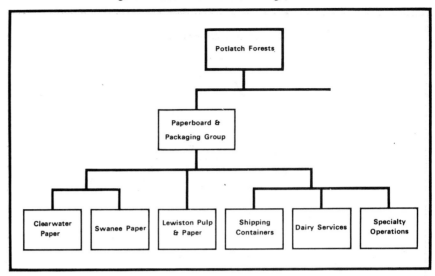

Figure 13. Consolidated Modelling Structure.

## WHAT IS THE BASIC CONCEPTUAL FRAMEWORK?

All of the models are simulation with the exception of one optimization model used by a large oil company. Planners have similarly been unanimous in their selections of deterministic rather than stochastic models because they were so much easier to develop, were understandable by management, and input variations can be handled on a case by case basis. Modellers have also found it advantageous to work from the general to the specific, from the top of the organization down to operations. Surprisingly, it is much easier to model a large firm at the corporate level than it is a small operation requiring a high order of accuracy and attendant data problems. The consolidated modelling framework follows the organizational structure (Figure 13).

## IS DATA AVAILABILITY A PROBLEM?

Yes, many firms have been restricted in the degree to which they can apply computerized corporate planning because the historical data has not been adequate to permit developing meaningful relationships between variables. The firms have not generally deferred modelling for this reason, however, but have built around the problem on the philosophy that decisions have to be made in any instance. The models have been kept general to avoid problems of this nature, and subsequently refined as the data became available.

## WHAT IS THE DISTINCTION BETWEEN MANAGEMENT INFORMATION SYSTEMS AND COMPUTERIZED CORPORATE PLANNING?

The two systems are often confused and, in some instances, the former is thought to be a prerequisite for the latter. MIS refers to a system for accumulating operating data on a real time basis and making it available on inquiry. The MIS system normally requires several years to install and handles data on a detailed unit basis, i.e. items in inventory. The planning system, in contrast, deals with approximately 10 per cent of the detail of the MIS system, i.e. product categories, and can be installed in months (Figure 14). The planning system derives its logic from the decision requirements of management and subsequently provides the specifications for the MIS system. Logically it precedes the MIS system. Hopefully the two systems will someday be linked, however, the problems are formidable and

### Figure 12. Cost Estimates.

| | Annual Turnover | |
| --- | --- | --- |
| | Small firm (£4m.) | Large firm (£400m.) |
| Installation cost | | |
| Modelling consulting | £3500 | £25000 |
| Training | 440 | 1300 |
| System subscription | 2000 | 3600 |
| | £5940 | £29900 |
| Average Yearly Cost | | |
| Computer terminals | £360 | £ 1800 |
| Communication | 120 | 600 |
| Computer usage | 1400 | 5000 |
| System rental | 3000 | 7200 |
| | £4880 | £14600 |

**Figure 14. Information Pyramid.**

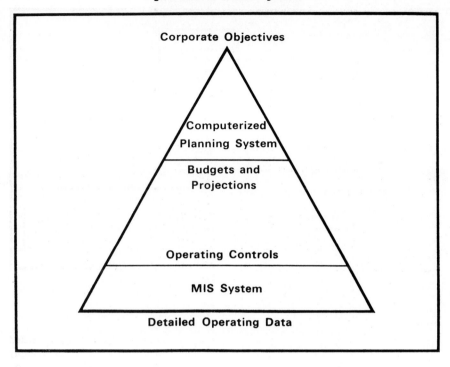

**Figure 15. Applications of Computerized Corporate Planning.**

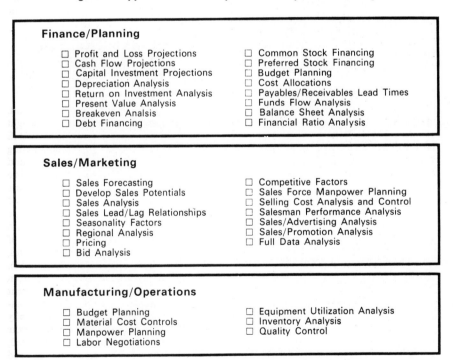

very few MIS systems are operational at this time. Fortunately, the need for integrating the two is not pressing since the planning system is not dependent upon absolute accuracy and immediate updating of data.

## ARE THE TIME-SHARE COMPUTER SYSTEMS ADEQUATE?

The technical requirements of the planning system are extreme as related to the computer systems on which they operate. Data security is more of a problem in Europe than in the U.S., but can be satisfactorily guaranteed in either instance. A major problem encountered by United States firms using time-share computers is the high load factor resulting in poor response time. This problem is particularly acute in the western United States, although it is difficult everywhere at peak hours of the day. Most systems do not have overlay capabilities and are hence unsatisfactory for complex modelling installations. Corporate planning systems use a great amount of CPU time which is expensive, especially in the United Kingdom. Back up computers are generally not available in Europe. The designers of computerized planning systems often find themselves faced with serious bugs in the manufacturers' software that have been unnoticed by less sophisticated users. Finally, data storage requirements are large in corporate planning systems and the user often finds the computer utility unreasonably expensive or storage facilities inadequate. In short, the time-share computer facilities constitute a serious problem and a limitation in the development of computerized planning systems.

## WHAT ARE THE MAJOR AREAS OF APPLICATION?

Computerized planning is expanding rapidly from financial modelling into marketing and operational applications with emphasis on pricing models (Figure 15). Tactical applications are becoming more important in the areas of labour negotiations, merger analysis, tax planning, cost estimating, etc. Companies with similar operations are beginning to share the cost of modelling as they have shared expenses for the computer and the software. The corporate simulation systems are being expanded to include suppliers, major customers, in fact the total industry. Management is becoming rapidly more sophisticated and losing the early fear of the computer. Unfortunately, some systems are being down graded to simple report generator applications and their decision interrogation capability ignored. Not withstanding the problems with time-shared computer systems, the trend is strongly away from batch systems to interactive capability.

## APPENDIX: COMPUTER SIMULATION IN EUROPE*

This is supposed to be an objective comment on Dr. Boulden's foregoing article. 'Objective', in the context, evidently means that the commentator is not biased (as the author might be) in favour of the author's own product. But to be objective is more difficult than that for any British specialist in simulation, who is confronted by a recently-devised American importation.

Boulden says: 'Modelling in Europe is controlled by the operations research groups and is still oriented to optimization, the search for the one best answer'. All I can say is that *we* in Britain have for many years regarded America as the home of the optimization–suboptimization 'hang-up'. As far as I am aware computer simulation technique was primarily developed in Britain 15 years ago, precisely with a view to exploring the phase-spaces of problem situations. And it was flourishing here at the time when the U.S.A. made Linear Programming solutions mandatory for those tendering for Government contracts. We remember the story about how the contracts for U.S. Army socks had to be totally redistributed, because the optimal solution saved about $10 over 1 year's supply. And did the British pioneers of simulation, Dr. K. D. Tocher at their head, work in vain?

Well, if British Steel saw the point of simulation, it is equally true to say that many other industries did not. And, as the French rapidly caught up, it was optimization rather than heuristic exploration that they pursued. When we go on to consider the extent to which the elaborate models built in this country have actually been used by senior management, we have to face up to some unpalatable facts. Oil made real money out of them; so did companies involved in food-mixes; and they said so. In my view, steel and coal and electricity made money out of them too—but they are dour industries, and said little. After that I could list several industries which *could* have profited greatly, even to the extent of saving their eventual demise, but lacked the managerial acumen to do so . . . In the realm of government, Professor Ragnar Frisch put Norway almost a generation ahead of the rest of the world (optimizing again though), and — much later though more ingeniously — Professor Richard Stone

*This Appendix is written by Professor Stafford Beer, Manchester Business School, University of Manchester.

gave Britain a model it did not know how to use.

So, I suppose Dr. Boulden is right. And that is especially evident when we come to the real point. The real point is that conversational simulations in the time-sharing mode are an order of magnitude more important (because more useful) than time-decoupled simulations ever were or could have been. They do not merely do all the sums for you; they enter the computer into a symbiotic relation with real-life managers. Again British workers had done something similar, though without the time-sharing facility; but their work was treated as experimental.

If we take a cool and fair look at the state of the art in Britain, what do we see? There is a long-established, mature, and advanced modelling tradition. At those points where it has broken through to managerial reality, it has been successful —sometimes wildly successful. As to real-time computer operation, Britain was not lagging there either. For example, the Stockbroker Computer Answering Network (SCAN), devised by Intinco in 1965, and later operated by International Data Highways, was on the air as a commercial proposition in early 1966—and that is a long time ago in terms of time-sharing. The software was just not available. Manufacturers claimed that it was; but it took irresponsible people, such as Charles Ross and Michael Gassman and their programmers of Intinco, to make it all work.

Despite all this impressive history, British managers do not as a matter of fact actually use *interactive* corporate models in their planning. This is what On-Line Decision is all about. Of course, few in-house computers are readily capable (through their operating systems) of the trick—and they are in any case weighed down by their routine load of batch work. So a special case has to be made to import a terminal from a time-sharing service. Then computer men themselves have to master a new kind of programming; and perhaps the very existence of sophisticated models prepared for batch operation represents an investment of time and skill which people are loath to abandon. Then again, as Boulden's article rightly stresses, there is the old excuse (it is nothing more) about there being an inadequate data base. I have never been able to understand this claim, and have never yet found it justified. The business, is being run; it is run on some data or other, however inadequate. To put those data into a model cannot conceivably make anything worse than it already is . . .

However seriously (or not) we take these

difficulties and mental blocks, I do not think the vital change in managerial practice adumbrated in this article can be resisted for long: the tool is too powerful. In *Cybernetics and Management*, written in 1958, I postulated a device which would continuously link the company and its environment through models of each; it would operate as a continuous learning system. In a *Postscript*, written in 1966 for a later edition, I added to the original sketch an exact description of the facility which Boulden's company now provides.

"Instead of sitting round a table arguing about 'the best thing to do', directors of the cybernetic firm will play games with the machine."

The tool has arrived. Managers and management scientists in Britain can be proud indeed of their achievements, and they can if they wish declare the On-Line package to be simplistic by comparison. There is nothing very special about the concepts, models programmes—or even the time-sharing prestidigitation. But there is nonetheless something else about it that is very special indeed. It works; it is used; it really happens. It seems that in a few years On-Line Decisions have a large number of industrial realities being simulated through their models. And the running cost seems to be roughly equivalent to the salary of a senior executive—in whatever size of enterprise you like.

I will leave my final comment in the form of a quotation by *Cybernetics and Management*—a quotation in print in 1958:

"At last we have a board-room tool worth having. It has taken a long time. Everyone in industry has sophisticated tools to help them do their jobs, from cyclotrons to tame economists, but general management remains armed with a board table, paper and pencils, and a bottle of whisky. It has a long hard night ahead. In principle, it is a god; if there is anything it needs it just asks for it. But in practice the information is not forthcoming, or it will take a month to get ready, or to measure it will start a strike. And so we operate by corporate faith. The future, it could so easily be the near future, will be better." ■

Today I say *Amen*.

# Experience with Corporate Simulation Models—A Survey

**Thomas H. Naylor**

Duke University and Social Systems, Inc.

and

**Horst Schauland**

Social Systems, Inc.

*In this article the authors argue that if corporate simulation models are going to help management meet their objectives then changes are necessary. These changes require that (i) the models should be more user oriented, (ii) there should be more emphasis on production modelling, (iii) there will be an increased use of optimization techniques linked to corporate models, (iv) there will be an increased effort to integrate finance, marketing and production, (v) the more sophisticated application will be concerned with the external environment and (vi) model builders should become more aware of the importance of corporate politics.*

## INTRODUCTION

THROUGH DIRECT PERSONAL CONTACT WE HAVE identified over 2000 corporations in the United States, Canada, and Europe who are either using, developing, or planning to develop some form of corporate planning model. In September of 1974 we mailed a 47-question questionnaire to 1881 corporations which were thought to be either using, developing, or planning to develop a corporate planning model. Our objectives were to ascertain (1) who is using corporate models, (2) why are they being used, (3) how are they used, (4) which resources are required, (5) which techniques and structures are being employed, (6) what are the costs and benefits, (7) what enhancements are planned, and (8) what does the future hold for corporate modeling. A total of 346 corporations

responded to the survey yielding a response rate of 19 per cent.

In 1969, George W. Gershefski conducted a similar survey of 1900 corporations of which 323 (17 per cent) responded.[1] At that time Gershefski was only able to identify 63 corporations (20 per cent of his sample) who claimed to be using or developing a corporate planning model. The results of our survey are summarized in Table 1.

In summary, 73 per cent of the firms in our sample were either using or developing a corporate model. Another 15 per cent were planning to develop such a model and only 12 per cent had no plans whatsoever to develop a planning model.

Of those firms which indicated they are using a corporate simulation model, 39 per cent claimed to have modeled the 'total company'. We suspect that this figure overstates the case and may reflect differences in interpretation as to what constitutes the 'total company'. In actual practice, relatively few firms have managed to integrate the financial, marketing, and production activities of the firm into a truly integrated corporate simulation model. Three notable exceptions to this rule are CIBA-GEIGY, IU International, and Anheuser-Busch. Each of these firms has successfully achieved the development and implementation of a total corporate simulation model. The CIBA-GEIGY model is probably the most sophisticated corporate simulation model in existence today. It is used extensively by corporate and division management to evaluate long range plans.

That 80 per cent of the firms which are using corporate planning models have modeled the financial structure of their business comes as no surprise to anyone. Indeed, the only surprising thing about that percentage is that it was not 100 per cent. Financial models are quite easy to develop,

**Table 1.  Number and Percentage of Firms Using Corporate Simulation Models.**

|  | Number of Corporations | Percentage |
|---|---|---|
| Using a Corporate Model | 213 | 62 |
| Developing a Corporate Model | 37 | 11 |
| Planning to Develop a Corporate Model | 55 | 15 |
| No Plans to Develop a Corporate Model | 41 | 12 |
| Total | 346 | 100 |

require a minimum amount of data, and can be validated against the firm's existing accounting structure. Some form of marketing model is being used by 41 per cent of the firms which have operational corporate planning models. This percentage reflects the fact that forecasting and econometric modeling techniques are not as well known to corporate planners as the more traditional tools of financial analysis. The production activities of the corporation have been modeled by 39 per cent of the firms which are users of corporate planning models. In most cases these production models are relatively straightforward activity analysis (cost accounting) models which reflect the cost of operating at different rates of output. However, CIBA-GEIGY and Anheuser-Busch make use of linear programming models to determine minimum cost production plans which are in turn linked to corporate financial models. The important point to realize is that while many firms (particularly the petroleum industry) make extensive use of mathematical programming models to run their refineries, relatively few of these mathematical programming models are linked into a corporate model.

## WHO IS USING CORPORATE MODELS?

We asked those firms which are using corporate simulation models to indicate who the actual users of the model are. The results are tabulated in Table 2. The table shows the percentage of firms in our sample for which a particular person is receiving and using information produced by the corporate model.

These results are indeed encouraging for they indicate that in approximately half of the corporations which are using corporate simulation models,

**Table 2.  People Receiving and Using Output from the Model.**

| User | Percentage |
|---|---|
| Vice-President of Finance | 55 |
| President | 46 |
| Controller | 46 |
| Executive Vice-President | 32 |
| Treasurer | 30 |
| Other Vice-President | 30 |
| Vice-President of Marketing | 29 |
| Chairman | 23 |
| Board Member | 21 |
| Vice President of Production | 21 |

the right people are receiving and actually using the output generated by the models. There is abundant evidence available to support the hypothesis that it is crucial to the success of any corporate modeling project to have the active participation of top management in both the problem definition phase of the project and the implementation stage. The fact that the president and senior financial executive of half of the firms using corporate models are among the users of these models bodes well for the future of corporate modeling.

Having established which people are involved in the use of corporate models, we now turn to the industries which are using them. Table 3 lists the users by major industrial classification.

Next we examine the relative size of the firms in our sample which are using corporate simulation models. We use total sales as a measure of the size of these corporations.

Although over half of the firms in our sample of corporate modeling users have sales in excess of $500m., it is interesting to note that 10 per cent of

**Table 3.  Firms Using Corporate Models Classified by Industry.**

| Industry | Number of Firms |
|---|---|
| Manufacturing | 64 |
| Banking and Finance | 30 |
| Regulated Industries (transportation, communications, utilities) | 20 |
| Service | 15 |
| Mining | 7 |
| Agriculture | 5 |
| Other | 18 |
| No Response | 54 |
| Total | 213 |

the users of corporate models have sales which are less than $100m. With the advent of timesharing computer languages which facilitate the development of corporate planning models, corporate modeling is now economically feasible for firms with sales less than $10m.

The geographic distribution of corporations which are employing corporate simulation models may also be of some interest. As can be seen in Table 5, firms using corporate models are spread rather evenly over the Midwest, Northeast, and South. Most of the Canadian firms using corporate models are located in or near Toronto and Montreal. (Table 5 only reflects the location of the corporate headquarters of the firms.)

**Table 4.   Sales of Firms Using Corporate Models.**

|  | Percentage |
|---|---|
| Under $50m. | 7 |
| $50m. to $100m. | 3 |
| $100m. to $250m. | 8 |
| $250m. to $500m. | 16 |
| $500m. to $1 billion | 21 |
| Over $1 billion | 38 |
| No response | 7 |
| Total | 100 |

**Table 5.   Geographic Location of Firms Using Corporate Models.**

| Location | Percentage |
|---|---|
| United States | |
| Midwest | 18 |
| Northeast | 17 |
| South | 14 |
| West | 7 |
| Canada | 12 |
| Europe | 5 |
| No Response | 27 |

Finally, some descriptive information of the people who filled out the questionnaire may help put the results of this survey in perspective. In response to the question 'What is your relationship to your firm's corporate model?' Fifty-two per cent of the respondents were users of the model, 69 per cent were model builders, and 29 per cent were sponsors of the project. As for the age distribution of the respondents, 26 per cent were under 30 years old, 49 per cent were between 31 and 40 years old, 17 per cent were between 41 and 50, and 5 per cent were between 51 and 60. None of the respondents were over 60 and 3 per cent chose not to reveal their age. The respondents were found to be members of the following professional organizations—The Institute of Management Science (TIMS) 31 per cent, Operations Research Society of America (ORSA) 18 per cent, North American Society for Corporate Planning 14 per cent, Planning Executives Institute 9 per cent, Association for

Computing Machinery 6 per cent, and Financial Executives Institute 3 per cent.

## WHY ARE THEY USED?

Financial applications dominate the list of reasons why corporations are using corporate planning models these days. Cash flow analysis, financial forecasting, balance sheet projections, financial analysis, pro forma financial reports, and profit planning are among the leading applications of corporate simulation models. Table 6 contains a summary list of existing applications of corporate models based on our survey results. The percentages denote the percentage of firms in our sample of users which make use of a particular application.

**Table 6.   Applications of Corporate Models.**

| Applications | Percentage |
|---|---|
| Cash Flow Analysis | 65 |
| Financial Forecasting | 65 |
| Balance Sheet Projections | 64 |
| Financial Analysis | 60 |
| Pro Forma Financial Reports | 55 |
| Profit Planning | 53 |
| Long-Term Forecasts | 50 |
| Budgeting | 47 |
| Sales Forecasts | 41 |
| Investment Analysis | 35 |
| Marketing Planning | 33 |
| Short-Term Forecasts | 33 |
| New Venture Analysis | 30 |
| Risk Analysis | 27 |
| Cost Projections | 27 |
| Merger-Acquisition Analysis | 26 |
| Cash Management | 24 |
| Price Projections | 23 |
| Financial Information System | 22 |
| Industry Forecasts | 20 |
| Market Share Analysis | 17 |
| Supply Forecasts | 13 |

## HOW ARE THEY USED?

Next we shall analyze the results of a series of questions aimed at determining how corporate models are used. Table 7 indicates that corporate simulation models are used most often (1) to evaluate alternative policies, (2) to provide financial projections, (3) to facilitate long-term planning. (4) to make decisions, and (5) to facilitate short-term planning.

**Table 7.   How Corporate Models are Used.**

| Use | Percentage |
|---|---|
| Evaluation of Policy Alternatives | 79 |
| Financial Projections | 75 |
| Long Term Planning | 73 |
| Decision Making | 58 |
| Short Term Planning | 56 |
| Preparation of Reports | 47 |
| Corporate Goal Setting | 46 |
| Analysis | 39 |
| Conformation of Other Analysis | 35 |

The time frame on which corporate models are based varies widely. Forty-five per cent of the corporate models in our sample are *annual* models, 5 per cent are *quarterly* models, 14 per cent are *monthly* models, and 33 per cent are some combination of the above. The average length of the planning horizon turned out to be 8 years for the firms in our sample. The frequency with which the model is used was found to vary from several times a day to annually. One third of the respondents indicated the model was used 'when necessary'.

**Table 8.    Frequency of Use of Corporate Model.**

| Frequency of Use | Percentage |
|---|---|
| Several Times a Day | 5 |
| Daily | 7 |
| Weekly | 9 |
| Monthly | 18 |
| Quarterly | 17 |
| Yearly | 8 |
| When Necessary | 33 |
| No Response | 3 |
| | 100 |

## RESOURCE REQUIREMENTS

Most of the existing corporate models (67 per cent) were developed in-house without any outside assistance from consultants, 25 per cent were developed in-house with outside consulting, and 8 per cent were purchased from an outside vendor.

Eighteen man-months was the average amount of effort required to develop models in-house without outside assistance. The average cost of these models was $82,752.

For those models which were developed in-house with the help of outside consultants, the average elapsed time required to complete the model was 10 months. The average cost for those models was $29,225.

In terms of computer hardware, 42 per cent of the models are run on in-house computing equipment, 37 per cent are run on an outside timesharing bureau, and 19 per cent run both in-house and on a timesharing bureau. Of the firms using corporate models in our sample, 62 per cent run their models in conversational mode while 56 per cent utilize the batch mode of computation. In our sample of firms using corporate models, 43 per cent ran these models on IBM computers, 5 per cent on UNIVAC, 4 per cent on Honeywell, 3 per cent on Xerox, 2 per cent on Burroughs, 1 per cent on Digital Equipment Corporation and 1 per cent on NCR.

FORTRAN is by far the most widely used computer language for programming corporate simulation models. Fifty per cent of the existing models were programmed in FORTRAN, 8 per cent in COBOL, 5 per cent in PL/1, 4 per cent in APL, 2 per cent in Assembler, and 1 per cent in DYNAMO. Another 26 per cent of the models were programmed in one of over 40 planning and budgeting languages which are available to facilitate the development and programming of corporate planning models. These include languages like PROPHIT II, PSG, SIMPLAN, and ORACLE. These languages tend to be much more user (management) oriented than scientific languages such as FORTRAN, APL, and PL/1. Although firms with sales less than, $100m. typically would not employ scientific programmers, it is possible to teach financial analysts a language like SIMPLAN or ORACLE in a matter of a few hours. With the availability of planning languages on timesharing bureaus, much smaller firms now find it economically feasible to develop and use corporate models.

Although econometric modeling techniques are not used very extensively even by the largest corporations in the United States, Canada, and Europe, we found that 57 per cent of the firms using corporate models subscribed to some national econometric forecasting service. In the United States these services include Wharton, Chase Econometrics, and DRI.

## MODEL STRUCTURE

In this section we shall summarize the features which characterize the logical structure of the corporate models which are presently in use. The vast majority (94 per cent) of these models are what management scientists call *deterministic* models. That is, they do not include any random or probabilistic variables. Models which incorporate one or more probability distributions for variables such as sales, costs, etc. are called *risk analysis* models. Only 6 per cent of the corporate models in our sample make use of risk analysis. This result is by no means surprising, since risk analysis models involve a host of statistical and computational complexities which one can avoid by using deterministic models.

Most (76 per cent) of the corporate planning models are *what if* models, i.e., models which simulate the effects of alternative managerial policies and assumptions about the firm's external environment. Only 4 per cent of the models in our sample were optimization models in which the goal was to maximize or minimize a single objective function such as profit or cost, respectively. However, 14 per cent of the models use both approaches. The remainder of the firms in our sample either did not respond to the question or use some other approach.

The average number of equations in the models in our sample was 545. The range varied from 20 equations to several thousand equations. Most of the equations are definitional equations which take the form of accounting identities. The average number of definitional equations was 445. The average number of behavioral (empirical) equations was only 86. Behavioral equations take the form of theories or hypotheses about the behavior of certain economic phenomena. They must be tested empirically and validated before they are incorporated into the model.

Twenty-nine per cent of the respondents described their models as a collection of independent single equations not related to one another. Another 36 per cent of the models were said to consist of a set of causally ordered (recursive) equations linked together over time. Only 16 per cent of these models were jointly determined (simultaneous) linear equation models. And 6 per cent were simultaneous non-linear equation models.

## FORECASTING TECHNIQUES

Many corporate simulation models incorporate some form of short term forecasting techniques particularly for sales and revenue projections. Table 9 indicates the extent to which forecasting routines have been utilized in the corporate models in our sample.

**Table 9.    Forecasting Techniques Used in Corporate Models.**

| Forecasting Technique | Percentage |
|---|---|
| Growth Rate | 50 |
| Linear Time Trend | 40 |
| Moving Average | 22 |
| Exponential Smoothing | 20 |
| Non-Linear Time Trend | 15 |
| Adaptive Forecasting | 9 |
| Box–Jenkins | 4 |

The conclusion from Table 9 is that the less complex forecasting techniques like simple growth rates, time trends, and moving averages are used more extensively than the more sophisticated techniques such as adaptive forecasting and Box–Jenkins techniques. Although time trends and exponential smoothing are relatively easy techniques to use and interpret, the Box–Jenkins technique is not a technique for amateurs. On the other hand, adaptive forecasting may yield forecasts which are equal to those produced by the Box–Jenkins method, but the technique is much easier to understand than Box–Jenkins.

## BENEFITS

As can be seen in Table 10, the major benefits which current users of corporate models have derived include: (1) ability to explore more alternatives, (2) better quality decision making, (3) more effective planning, (4) better understanding of the business, and (5) faster decision making.

**Table 10.    Benefits of Corporate Models.**

| Benefits | Percentage |
|---|---|
| Able to Explore More Alternatives | 78 |
| Better Quality Decision Making | 72 |
| More Effective Planning | 65 |
| Better Understanding of the Business | 50 |
| Faster Decision Making | 48 |
| More Timely Information | 44 |
| More Accurate Forecasts | 38 |
| Cost Savings | 28 |
| No Benefits | 4 |

## LIMITATIONS

Opinions about the limitations of corporate models do not appear to be as intense or as well defined as opinions about the benefits of these models. The three shortcomings mentioned most often were: (1) lack of flexibility, (2) poor documentation, and (3) excessive input data requirements.

## IMPORTANT FEATURES

Also included in our survey was a question about 'Which methods and techniques do you need most in your model building efforts?' The answers generated by this question can provide a basis for the design of future corporate models. Table 12 contains a list of the features which were mentioned most often.

## THE POLITICS OF CORPORATE MODEL BUILDING

Crucial to the successful implementation of any corporate simulation model is the political support

**Table 11. Shortcomings of Corporate Models.**

| Shortcomings | Percentage |
|---|---|
| Is Not Flexible Enough | 25 |
| Poorly Documented | 23 |
| Requires Too Much Input Data | 23 |
| Output Format is Inflexible | 11 |
| Took Too Long to Develop | 11 |
| Running Cost is Too High | 9 |
| No Shortcomings | 9 |
| Development Cost Was Too High | 8 |
| Model Users Cannot Understand Model Development | 8 |
| Analytic Process is Not Understandable | 5 |
| Output is Not Detailed Enough | 4 |
| Not User-Oriented | 3 |
| Results are Obviously Inaccurate | 3 |
| Output is Too Detailed | 3 |
| Does Not Model What is Intended | 2 |

**Table 12. Important Features of Corporate Models.**

| Features | Percentage |
|---|---|
| Sensitivity Analysis | 52 |
| Simple Database Utilization | 50 |
| Flexible Report Generation | 50 |
| Accounting Functions | 39 |
| Simple Commands | 37 |
| Risk Analysis | 36 |
| Least Squares Estimation | 33 |
| Seasonal Adjustment | 30 |
| Graphics | 28 |
| Linear Programming | 25 |
| Simultaneous System of Equations | 25 |
| Recursive System of Equations | 24 |
| Exponential Smoothing | 22 |
| Frequency Distributions, Histograms, or Bar Charts | 22 |
| Linear, Quadratic, and Logarithmic Trend Lines | 19 |
| Security | 15 |
| Analysis of Variance | 12 |
| Box–Jenkins Method | 11 |
| Adaptive Smoothing | 10 |
| Non-Linear Programming and Optimization | 10 |
| Two Stage Least Squares Estimation | 9 |
| Non-Linear Least Squares Estimation | 8 |
| Scatter Diagrams | 5 |
| Polynomial Distributed Lag Estimation | 5 |

of top management. Although suitable models and computer software are necessary for the success of corporate modeling, they are by no means sufficient. If the president of the company or at least the vice-president of finance is not fully committed to use of a corporate model, then the results are not likely to be taken seriously and the model will see only limited use.

To get some feeling for the political environment in the firms where corporate modeling is being used, we asked a series of attitudinal questions concerning the interest of management in the corporate modeling activities of their firm. Table 13 contains a summary of the attitudes expressed by the firms in our sample. The findings displayed in Table 13 seem to imply that the corporate models included in our survey enjoy a relatively high degree of political support on the part of management. In 60 per cent of the firms which are using corporate models top management is 'somewhat interested' in corporate modeling while another 30 per cent are 'very interested'. On the other hand, the degree of interest in corporate modeling expressed by planning departments and finance is even higher.

Another political consideration which can prove to be important is the question of which department is responsible for the development of a corporate model. Table 14 indicates that although the planning department is the department which most often has the responsibility for developing the model, there is a fairly even spread among other companies which have chosen either finance, operations research, or management science as the department responsible for development of the model.

If a company has centralized corporate planning and if the director or vice-president of corporate planning reports to the president, then it is difficult to find any compelling reason why development of a corporate planning model should be under the auspices of any other department. It is interesting to note, however, that in a number of corporations, the control of the corporate model has been perceived as an important source of political power. As a result, one frequently finds serious conflicts and rivalries among various departments competing for control of the corporate model.

## THE FUTURE OF CORPORATE MODELING

As we indicated in the introduction, the number of firms using of developing corporate simulation

**Table 13. Attitudes of Management Towards Corporate Modeling.**

|  | Very Interested (per cent) | Somewhat Interested (per cent) | Indifferent (per cent) | Not at All Interested (per cent) | No Response (per cent) |
|---|---|---|---|---|---|
| Top Management | 30 | 60 | 8 | 1 | 1 |
| Planning | 57 | 22 | 4 | 1 | 6 |
| Finance | 54 | 37 | 5 | 3 | 1 |
| Marketing | 23 | 39 | 24 | 8 | 6 |
| Production | 15 | 31 | 31 | 8 | 15 |
| Data Processing | 31 | 24 | 26 | 9 | 10 |

**Table 14.   Departments Responsible for Corporate Model Development.**

| Department Responsible | Percentage |
|---|---|
| Corporate Planning | 27 |
| Finance | 16 |
| Operations Research | 15 |
| Other | 13 |
| Management Science | 12 |
| Data Processing | 7 |
| Management Information Systems | 7 |
| Marketing | 3 |
| | 100 |

models has increased from less than 100 in 1969 to over 2000 in 1975. In a field characterized by such dramatic growth in such a short period of time, one can anticipate rapid changes in both the technology and application of corporate models over the next 10 years.

Before speculating about the future of corporate modeling, it may be useful to go beyond the results of our survey and attempt to identify a number of reasons why so many firms are turning to the use of corporate planning models. The reasons people are turning to corporate planning models are almost identical to the reasons for implementing centralized corporate planning. The essence of corporate planning is risk and uncertainty. The degree of risk and uncertainty present in the external environment faced by most corporations is perhaps at an all time high. Nearly every firm in the United States is facing the following problems:

(1) Energy.
(2) Inflation.
(3) Liquidity Crunch.
(4) Shortages.
(5) Declining Productivity.
(6) Economic Uncertainty.

Faced with some combination of all of these problems, corporations are looking for new technologies such as computer simulation models which enable them to evaluate the impact of alternative policies, opportunities, and external events on the performance of the entire corporation.

If corporate simulation models are going to help management meet the challenges and the opportunities generated by the events described above, then some changes must necessarily take place in the theory and application of corporate simulation models.

First, there seems to be a definite need to make corporate simulation models more user-oriented. If top management is going to be motivated to participate in the development of a corporate model and to make use of the model once it has been completed, then both the model and the modeling language must be relatively easy to understand. Corporate models which have been written in scientific programming languages like FORTRAN and APL do not tend to be very user-oriented. A number

of the new planning and budgeting languages like PROPHIT II and SIMPLAN are highly user-oriented and greatly facilitate both the conceptualization and the coding of corporate simulation models.

Second, we anticipate that the use of production planning models linked into an overall corporate simulation model will become increasingly important. The energy crisis, shortages, and problems of declining productivity, necessarily imply that greater attention will be given to production modeling than has been the case in the past.

Third, some firms may soon begin experimenting with the use of optimization techniques linked to corporate planning models. This linkage is likely to occur in two important areas. The most obvious area is in production planning where mathematical programming routines can be used to generate the minimum cost production plans associated with given demand forecast. In addition, some firms are beginning to experiment with the use of goal programming and portfolio optimization models to assist in the allocation of resources among alternative divisions or strategic business units in the firm.

Fourth, although relatively few firms have successfully integrated finance, marketing, and production into a single overall corporate simulation model, there is every indication that we will see an increasing number of firms moving in this direction. In the past, these types of linkages were very cumbersome to do in conventional scientific programming languages. It was difficult to build in adaptability and flexibility. Some of the new corporate simulation languages greatly simplify the integration of finance, marketing, and production into a single corporate simulation model.

Fifth, a number of firms such as Xerox and General Electric are now beginning to experiment with models of the external environment as well as internal corporate planning models. We see this type of modeling becoming much more important during the next decade. A series of global, economic, political, social, and environmental problems have given rise to a new breed of corporate futurists.

Sixth, we believe that both model builders and users of corporate simulation models are becoming increasingly aware of the importance of corporate politics in the successful implementation of a corporate planning model. Model builders are finally learning to speak the language of top management. Top management has learned to ask the right questions. ■

**REFERENCE**

(1) George W. Gershefski, Corporate Models—The State of the Art, *Managerial Planning*, November–December (1969) and reprinted in *Management Science*, February (1970) and *Corporate Simulation Models*, Albert N. Schrieber (ed.), Graduate School of Business, University of Washington, Seattle, Washington (1970).

# Corporate Planning Using Government Information Systems

*Hirohide Hinomoto and James M. Reddy**

*Agencies of the U.S. Government collect large quantities of data some of which are useful for private firms (eg) in developing long-range plans. However a problem arises in that considerable time may elapse before the data is published. As a result it often becomes too old for companies to use if they are operating in dynamic markets.*

*The information system discussed in this paper (relating to the Fertilizer industry) bypasses this delay. It enables a private firm to have direct access to the files maintained by the National Fertilizer Development Centre of TVA.*

## Introduction

In 1974, a fertilizer producer developed a unique information system for long range planning that obtained data directly from on-line computer files maintained and updated by a government agency through a commercial time-sharing network. At that time such an arrangement was unheard of in the fertilizer industry and perhaps in most other industries. The fertilizer producer was the Swift Agricultural Chemical Company, located in Chicago, Illinois, and the government agency was the National Fertilizer Development Center of the Tennessee Valley Authority (TVA), located in Muscle Shoals, Alabama.

The ability of the information system to have direct access to the TVA files gave Swift two advantages. First, Swift could obtain necessary data more timely than before. Previously, some of these data had to be obtained from *World Fertilizer Market Review and Outlook*, a biennial report of TVA, and others from *Annual Fertilizer Review*, an annual report of the United Nations' Farm and Agriculture Organization (FAO). Second, since data were captured directly from the computer files, they could be manipulated and converted to any desired form inside the computer system

without being processed before they were printed out by a terminal at Swift.

The implication of the development of this information system seems significant to both public and private planners who are usually in need of information not available within their organizations. Most information systems maintained by a typical organization are to produce information essential to its daily operation. Data collected for this purpose may be used to control the performances of organizational functions or to make short-run decisions regarding these functions. But such data alone are not sufficient for long range planning. For long range planning purposes, an organization usually needs data concerning the trend of the entire market or industry, the trend of demand for its services or products, and its relative positions in the market or industry with regard to the volume of production or the value of sales. Normally, collecting these data on a continuous basis is either impractical or too costly for most private organizations.

On the other hand, various government agencies are engaged in collecting and maintaining a great variety of data including those that are useful to private and public planners. For example, the data may include those of economic activities in the entire industry or market in the U.S.A. and sometimes in the world. These data may eventually be published in government publications. But the published data are often too old to be useful for a firm operating in dynamic market. It may be reasonable to assume that these data are stored in computer files. If these were on-line computer files, it would be possible for other organizations to have direct access to them under government authorization through a commercial computer network, as is done by Swift. Such an arrangement would enable private and public planners to acquire a variety of useful data in an economic way. In this respect, the information system developed by Swift has merely touched the tip of an iceberg that has hitherto been mostly unexploited.

### The Fertilizer Business
The fertilizer business is subject to highly seasonal and cyclical fluctuations. To understand these fluctuations, a

---

*Professor Hinomoto is at the University of Illinois. James Reddy is with the Swift Agricultural Chemical Company.

firm needs two different types of information. During the fertilizer selling season, it is essential for a firm to have daily information on types of fertilizers sold, and areas and volumes of these sales. Information in this detail or timeliness is not needed for long range planning, but a more aggregate type of information regarding such matters as consumption trends, production plans, or expansion plans.

Basic fertilizer materials contain primarily one of the three main plant nutrients—nitrogen, phosphorus, and potassium. Nitrogen is supplied in the form of ammonia produced mainly from natural gas, whereas phosphorus and potassium are obtained mainly from phosphate and potash ores. While production of ammonia is virtually unlimited, phosphate and potash ores are found in a limited number of deposits in the world. The major deposits of phosphate ores are located in three regions: Florida and other locations of the United States represent about 30 per cent of the world's known reserves; North African mines in Tunisia, Algeria, and Morocco make up about 50 per cent of the world's reserves; and about 15 per cent is found in the Kola Peninsula in north-western Russia. Major potash deposits are located in western U.S., Canada, Central Europe, and Russia.

Being a truly international commodity, the supply or demand for fertilizer in one part of the world affects those in other parts. Therefore, before undertaking a major project such as expansion of mining capacity that may cost in excess of $100m, a firm should be informed of the plans of its competitors. But exchanging information with domestic competitors is complicated by both government regulations and normal competitive secrecy. Gaining information from foreign competitors is very expensive at best or often impractical. Many of these problems may be resolved if a government agency collects and disseminates the information, or exchanges the information with other countries.

Tennessee Valley Authority was created by congress in 1933 to help develop all resources in the Tennessee Valley Region in a single comprehensive program. While most TVA activities are confined to the valley, its responsibility for fertilizer research, development, and education is nationwide. These fertilizer activities are carried out at the National Fertilizer Development Center in Muscle Shoals, Alabama. The center represents the United States in the work of the statistical committee of the United Nations Food and Agricultural Organization (FAO). One of the reports published by TVA is its biennial *World Fertilizer Market Review and Outlook* that contains historical data and projections made by TVA for consumption, capacity, production, export and import for the three primary fertilizer nutrients and some of the major intermediate products of these nutrients.

One day in the spring of 1974, the director of planning at Swift was looking at tables in the latest issue of *World Fertilizer Review and Outlook* that had just come to his desk. He found information contained in the report useful, but was also greatly disappointed by the fact that much of the information was too old to be used for plans covering the immediate future in the dynamic fertilizer business. He conjectured that TVA might maintain some kinds of files to publish the report and these files might contain more recent data. To investigate the availability of such data, the director sent a representative to the TVA Center in June 1974.

*Direct Use of TVA Files*
Initially, Swift was interested in making an arrangement for obtaining typed or printed copies of data available in TVA's files whenever needs arose. However, the company had no idea about the manner in which TVA maintained the fertilizer data and the full extent of the data itself. Upon his arrival at the centre, the representative from the company learned that TVA's activity in collecting data on fertilizer was much more comprehensive than was presumed previously.

TVA maintained two files containing data related to the use of fertilizer in the world. One file contained the capacity of every known fertilizer plant in the world and the main products produced by the plant. The second file contained fertilizer production, consumption, import, and export data on all countries of the world since 1962. Both files were stored in a computer system at the processing center of the GE timesharing system in Rockville, Maryland. They were constantly updated by TVA's full time staff through their own terminal with information obtained from 30 periodicals and data supplied by FAO members at their annual meetings.

Specifically, the plant file stores data on the following details of about 5000 plants owned by some 1400 companies in the world: (1) country name, one of the 155 countries represented in FAO, (2) economic region, one of the 11 economic regions, (3) company name, (4) location in the country, (5) product name, one of the 47 different fertilizer products, (6) industry type, one of the six types including chemical industry, cooperative fertilizer industry, petrochemical industry, governments, others, and by-products, (7) plant characteristics regarding present operational status, year of starting operation, design capacity, and last updating date.

The second of the TVA files contains data collected and used by FAO for the publication of the *Annual Fertilizer Review*. These are statistical data on production, consumption, import and export volumes in metric tons for ten nitrogen intermediates, six phosphate intermediates, and six potash intermediates, in all countries of the world since 1962. The file is updated once a year with information supplied by FAO member countries at the annual meeting, but corrections and revisions to its data are made throughout the year.

The representative of Swift and TVA's staff discussed various alternatives to make the data available to Swift. Both parties considered one particular alternative most interesting and needing further investigation. It was an arrangement in which Swift was to become a direct user of the TVA files through the GE timesharing system. Swift's management considered this arrangement most useful and immediately initiated formal negotiations with both GE and TVA to make it a reality. In the early July of 1974, the company became a user of the GE timesharing system with 'Read Only' access to the TVA files.

The net result of this arrangement was an information system in which on-line files were maintained and updated by TVA at one end in Muscle Shoals, and directly used by Swift at the other end in Chicago, as is schematically shown in Figure 1. Simultaneous with the above arrangement, Swift was authorized to use several programs developed by TVA.

*Forecasting System*
Of the various types of useful information that could be produced from data available in the TVA files, the most urgent one for Swift was future demand for fertilizer in various countries of the world.

In developed countries, the farmer may decide the use of a fertilizer product, taking into consideration factors such as fertilizer price, farm products' expected prices, yields, and crop areas. Since the values of these factors are different in different regions of a country, predicting the short-run domestic demand requires collecting a huge volume of regional data that would be beyond the capability of most individual firms. In the long run, the problem becomes worse because of the interaction between the domestic market and the international market.

For less developed countries, forecasting fertilizer demand is very difficult because of lack of useful data. FAO publications that provide data since 1962 are the only sources of agricultural data for most countries. Further, the data for many of the countries are incomplete. Even if a complete set of data were available for a country, a little over 10 observation points since 1962 would be hardly adequate for developing a meaningful demand function in these years of rapid changes in world economy.

The difficulty of developing demand functions for fertilizers did not alter the urgent needs of Swift for information on domestic and foreign demands for fertilizer. As one of the reasons for the needs, it would take 3 years to build a new plant and the firm had to know demand projections for at least several years beyond that period in order to justify the construction. It was exactly the lack of such systematic forecasting methods that led fertilizer companies to increase production facilities and glut the market in the mid-1960s. As a result, all these firms suffered losses in operation. Faced with the irreconcilable conditions, the need for a forecasting method and the lack of useful data, Swift's conclusion was to develop a trend curve by regression analysis of the available data rather than developing a demand function, assuming that the future trend was given by an extrapolation of the regression line.

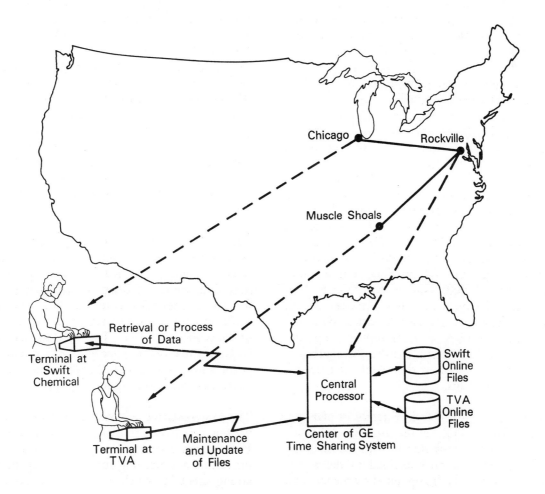

Figure 1

According to one proposition, fertilizer consumption in a market may be given by a stretched S shaped curve, composed of three phases of fertilizer use. The first phase is given by an accelerated increase applicable to the early stage of fertilizer use. Second phase is given by a straight-line increase representing a stage of steady growth. The third phase is given by a decelerating increase representing a stage of maturity. This proposition, however, was not verified by the FAO data. For one thing, the data on mature economic regions such as North America and West Europe still showed an accelerated increase while economic regions such as developing Asia showed a decelerated increase. Obviously, the proposition is too simple to explain the complex behavior of fertilizer consumption in any country.

The actual determination of the consumption trend of each economic region was done by using a polynomial regression program. Only linear or quadratic regression lines were obtained by the program. A higher degree polynomial regression was not used, because it tended to produce an unrealistically sharp upturn or downturn along a few last data points toward the end of the sample period. Finally, it was decided to represent the consumption trend of each economic region by one of the following three regression lines: a linear regression line representing a constant increase, a quadratic regression line representing an accelerated increase, and the average of two regression lines representing a decelerated increase* given by the following (1), (2), and (3), respectively:

$$Y = a_0 + a_1 X \tag{1}$$

$$Y = b_0 + b_1 X + b_2 X^2 \tag{2}$$

$$Y = \tfrac{1}{2}(a_0 + b_0) + \tfrac{1}{2}(a_1 + b_1)X + \tfrac{1}{2}b_2 X^2 \tag{3}$$

Using the consumption trend line obtained for each economic region, estimated consumptions for eight future years were computed along with their upper and lower points at a 95 per cent statistical confidence level. This computation was performed for each principal nutrient group—nitrogen, phosphate, and potash. Then the total consumption of each nutrient group was allocated to individual products constituting the group; and their upper and lower estimates were also made.

On the supply side, the volume of future production by product and country was estimated by combining past production data stored in the FAO file, the past rate of operation of each plant stored in the TVA plant capacity file, and data on shipping losses, and non-fertilizer uses in the past. As in the consumption forecast, an upper and a lower values of supply were

projected by getting a high and a low estimate of the operating rate based on the past experience.

The estimated consumption and production of values produced by the method outlined above gave Swift information which was useful for long range planning. In the short run, however, economic and other disturbances could cause the actual consumption and production sufficiently deviant from the long-run trends. For example, the oil price increase in late 1973 caused a traumatic increase in fertilizer prices. Because of this price increase combined with world-wide recession, the world fertilizer consumption dropped sharply in 1975 and is yet to rebound to its long-run trend.

Faced with these short-run disturbances, Swift needed to make realistic adjustments to short-term estimates of fertilizer consumption and production obtained from the long-term trends. The company used the Delphi method to make such adjustments. In this method, knowledgeable managers within the company were first given the consumption and operating rate figures estimated by the long-run trends and those estimated by trade journals and other knowledgeable sources, and then they were asked to make their estimates of changes in trend values. The estimates thus produced were summarized and returned to the managers for their comments. This process was repeated until their consensus was reached. The estimates of changes in consensus were then applied to the long-run trend formulas determined by past data in order to obtain final consumption and production estimates for the coming 3 years.

## Conclusion

The long range information system developed at the Swift Agricultural Chemical Company is unique in that it crosses the boundary between TVA's National Fertilizer Development Center, a public agency, and Swift, a private company. On the one hand, TVA, for its own use, maintains and updates online computer files containing economic data on fertilizer production, consumption, export and import as well as data on the characteristics of any known fertilizer plant in the world. On the other hand, Swift uses data contained in those files in any manner it desires. The arrangement therefore, completely relieves Swift of the tedious tasks of maintaining and updating the source data, and enables the company to concentrate on the use of these data.

Using TVA's data, the company has developed an information system for long range planning purposes. For short-run operational decisions, however, consumption estimates given by the information system are adjusted by correction factors agreed on by a group of knowledgeable managers. Since its creation, the information system has found various unanticipated uses. To mention one, the listing of fertilizer production capability or consumption of a foreign country has been found to be useful in negotiating business with the

---

*When the past consumption data are fitted with a quadratic curve with a positive but less-than-linear increase, the curve tends to forecast consumptions decreasing with time in future years. This forecasting is considered unrealistic for most countries. The problem is resolved in most cases by replacing the quadratic trend curve in (2) by an average of the linear and quadratic trend curves given by (3).

country. In one case, representatives of one country were impressed by the fact that Swift had access to better information of the country's fertilizer plants than that available to them.

The success of the information system developed at Swift has prompted over 30 companies in the U.S., France, Italy, Israel, Japan and Korea to follow suit by establishing or planning to establish direct access to the TVA files. Royalties paid by these users defray the cost of collecting data by TVA. More importantly, they now lend direct help to TVA by supplying more accurate and timely data that are otherwise unavailable to the agency.

# PART THREE

# Managing Information Technology for Strategic Impact

# Key Issues in Managing Information

*Richard Sizer, CEng, FIEE, FBCS*

In this article data, information and state of knowledge are described and then related to the decision-making process. The theme that data is a valuable commodity needing management is then developed. Then follows a section on computers, organizational policies and central and distributed processing. Some contractual aspects relating to procurement are described. Examples are given of actual applications in British industry, followed by discussion of two different issues, namely privacy and computer crime. The author draws the conclusion that 'information' per se is a personal, corporate and management asset which needs proper understanding and management in the computer era.

## 1. Introduction

It is not sufficient to use the word 'information' *per se* in order to study the management of information as a corporate resource. This paper proposes three component parts—data, information and state of knowledge (of the peruser of information). The distinction between the three can be illustrated by the following historical example.

In 1815 at the time of the Battle of Waterloo Nathan Rothschild realized that the result of the Battle would have a significant effect on the value of British Government bonds. He therefore devised a scheme to learn the outcome of the Battle well ahead of others. The scheme was based on a fast messenger service (and is alleged to have been costly for the time). However, the outlay was worth it as during the brief time in which he had a monopoly on the information (that the British had won) he made a fortune through bond dealings. This story (not apocryphal) has been told many times but for our present purposes it is necessary to make assumptions about the method by which the information was conveyed.

Perhaps, for example, there was a need to keep the content of the message secure so far as the messengers were concerned (who would no doubt have been skilled horsemen) so it may well have been coded. During the journey across the English Channel, being closer to the stock market in London, an even greater degree of security would have been necessary in case others had learned of the plan, knew the code (if one existed) and had made plans to intercept the message. Another assumption is that the message itself would have consisted of characters (data) written on a piece of paper sealed in a packet. The data became information only when perused by the eyes of Rothschild. As a result of the information his state of knowledge was changed, he made his decision and made a fortune.

Information has always been one of the main ingredients of business processes and forms the basis of all decision-making whether in a corporate or personal sense (as with Rothschild). In a military context the term 'intelligence' is used but amounts to the same thing: usually in a conflict the side with the better intelligence wins.

Computers have had and are having a profound effect on 'information' and the manner in which it is transmitted, presented, assimilated and used for a given purpose—even such purposes as crime and invasion of personal privacy. Only recently has the effect of computers on matters of this kind been made a subject in its own right.

The paper deals with the above aspects as well as the political effect of procurement within an organization. Surprisingly intense conflicts can be generated which cannot be attributed purely to the capital cost of the equipment being procured. Argument can become highly emotional, biased and generate enormous pressures on the individuals concerned.

Richard Sizer has been active in computing since 1957. He is Vice Chairman of the Professional Board at the BCS, U.K. representative on CECUA (Social Aspects); European Editor of 'Information Age' (Butterworth) and with Alistair Kelman, author of 'Computer in Court' (Gower) which deals with the validity of computer-generated evidence.
His address is: 26 Avenue Road, Farnborough, Hants. GU14 7BL, U.K.

Such situations defy rigorous analysis in most cases but it is a reasonable assumption to make that people are recognizing (implicitly or explicitly depending upon their background, experience and knowledge) that a computer can be a centre of information and that the 'owner' can become powerful unless steps are taken to set up a proper managerial control of the source of power.

Sections of the paper deal with practical aspects of information and illustrate some of the theoretical arguments developed earlier. Topics mentioned are contractual matters; three examples of information systems in British industry; privacy and security; computer-based crime.

## 2. Data Information and Knowledge

Data has always been a part of human activity. In ancient civilizations its storage and interpretation were often in the hands of an elite body. For example in the Inca civilization (sometimes referred to as a benevolent dictatorship) the priesthood had the monopoly of the code (knots on ropes of different colours called, collectively, quipu) and hence the aims and objectives of the Inca nation as only the priests were able to 'read' the quipu. In contrast, in modern society, although in certain cases concealment is practised, the codes (the alphabet) are usually known to all and data proliferates.

Information is comprised of data but is itself intangible. It cannot be stolen; if Rothschild had used a piece of paper and it had been stolen en route the thief could have been charged only with the theft of the paper. The information conveyed by data written on the paper though of considerable potential value counted for nothing in itself.

Information (in the computer context comprised of data in mechanical and electronic form in order to be able to be processed by a computer) appears in eye-readable form such as characters on the screen of a visual display unit (vdu). At this stage it has already been converted into characters which can be read and understood by the human being. (Within the computer the characters are in a different code which the machine can understand but the difference between the two codes is one of detail rather than principle.)

Data and information are clearly distinguishable from each other. Data has finite form and has to be perused in order that information can be gleaned from it which may or may not change the state of knowledge of the individual. Data and hence information can be communicated; data by a communication system which nowadays might be lengths of wire or light beams; information orally after, say, observation or perusal of data. Computers have added new dimensions of great

significance—one is the speed with which data appears at a given place and the consequent speed with which the information content has to be gleaned. The other is the volume of data. The speed and volume are so great that they break down patterns of human behaviour by overwhelming the decision-making process. Imagine for example the effect on the Inca priesthood and civilization if, as in the tale of the Sorcerer's Apprentice, the numbers of quipu multiplied a thousand-fold overnight: the whole process of government would probably have halted because of the inability of the priesthood to handle the data and absorb the information.

However, speed and volume are only two of the significant factors attributable to computers. Two others are accuracy and timeliness of data. The fact that data may be intrinsically highly accurate will count for little if, in an environment of objective competitiveness, it is presented later than data from within a competing organization. The timely presentation of processed data is dependent on the data communication and processing resources being adequate for a given task. The information-gleaning stage and the associated change of knowledge in the individual concerned take time; both follow serially the highly mechanized data processing stage. We will now examine the impact of information on decision-making.

A decision is based on an item of information which changes the state of knowledge of the individual concerned. The information can be good or bad—terms which are not necessarily synonymous with correct and incorrect. An analogy with the process of photography may make clear the distinction between good, bad, correct and incorrect. A bad-poor quality-photograph may record reality but may be so out of focus that the information content is virtually nil or misleading (bad). Although it is probably always true that incorrect data results in bad information (and a bad decision unless luck plays a part), it does not always follow that correct data results in good information because value judgments may arise; paradoxically, whilst the data may be of excellent quality in that it is highly accurate, the information content may be unwelcome at that moment in time or politically unacceptable. In the computer context, the data may be processed in too great a volume for it to be assimilated (in time for the given purpose); as information it may be politically contentious but, due to the prolific and impartial nature of computers where output is concerned, widely and embarrassingly distributed.

Most decisions are made on the basis of imperfect information for, at a given moment in time, the decision-maker can never know with certainty how perfect is the information on which he is acting. This can only be judged at some time later. Most decision-making is an iterative process; a threshold value is established where the quality of the information is judged adequate for the individual concerned to make a decision. Computers used properly can aid this iterative process but both volume of data and its timeliness have to be 'tuned' to the environment. Timely iteration implies timely processing which in turn means timely access to data and the processing power. Getting the volume right implies a systematic appreciation of the function and purpose of the activity.

## 3. The Need for Data Management

Data are a commodity which requires management in much the same way as any large stockholding has to be managed. There has to be a central 'filing system' so that items can be uniquely stored, located, retrieved, updated and transferred. Additionally there are its format, 'language', accuracy, relevancy, compatibility (with other data), ownership, rights of access, data identity, security classification, associative relationships with other data, who possess the authority to remove or amend data items, and so on.

Nearly all these features apply to both manually-stored and computer-based data. Whilst manual systems can be run inefficiently and result in business inefficiency, the effect is not often catastrophic. It is only in the context of computers that the scale of the mis-management problem becomes large enough for the effect on business efficiency to be serious to the point where a business activity can be brought to a halt by mismanaged and inadequate computing facilities.

## 4. Computers and Organizational Structure

The arguments concerning centralized, dispersed or distributed computing have taken place over the last few years. Some organizations have already abolished their older central computing facilities and adopted distributed data processing with communication by networks. In some cases these have been shown to be cost effective whilst in other cases the effect on the organization has been counterproductive and they have failed to function efficiently and economically.

The author showed elsewhere[1] that at a basic accounting level the minicomputer—the type of machine usually considered in a network or distributed context—whilst cheap (relatively) as a stand-alone item of equipment in a small organization, can be relatively expensive when large numbers are acquired on a laissez-faire basis by larger organizations. Sullivan[2] in a later study takes the matter further and shows that the annual cost (per mini) of running an application, is approximately double the original capital cost. He gives as an example, the processing cost of an application on

a central facility of $156,000 as opposed to $285,625 for processing the same application on a distributed mini.

Comparisons at one time were made between the computer and the human brain—unrewarding in the author's view because comparison was made in terms of power instead of (as is the theme of this paper) information processing. The author believes this to be the more relevant comparison particularly in terms of distributed mini computers, main-frames and communications. For example in chronological development of the human species the central nervous system is believed to have evolved before the brain which is not a single computer but a hierarchy of computer-like elements.[3]

Functionally these represent different decision-making levels. According to Beer[3] the threshold activity decides whether a particular item of information needs to be referred to the next level up. Simple decisions (reflex actions) take place at a low level as compared with conscious thought which is at the higher level. There are safeguards to prevent certain reflex actions being stopped by thought processes. This brief analysis shows how we have, by and large, failed to use computers effectively. Most of them have been at an ill-defined or unplanned managerial level. The central computer (or distributed minicomputers) have become overloaded in the corporate information-handling process; very few as at present im-plemented have the brain's threshold feature and 'reflex' protection mechanisms. Data communi-cation systems and the corresponding structure to deal with stimuli have been developed only as the need has been demonstrated usually by chaos—the reverse of the order which took place in natural evolution.

In the particular context of distributed processing the common mistake has been to assume that distributed processing implies distributed intelli-gence. However, some organizations have decen-tralized computing elements but not in intelligence terms—a strong centralized direction of policy has remained and it appears from the evidence available that these might have been the successful ones. Those who have diversified and decentralized computing but leaving no centralized intelligence are those which appear to have run into the problems already referred to.

## 5. Computers and Organizational Politics

Several people argue that computers cause interest to be concentrated more on internal politics than on the actual achievements which can be obtained from their use. For example Laudon[4] maintains that a new computer system becomes a political instrument and will be selected to a set of criteria which fit the shades of political forces in an organization reflecting conflicts and coalitions.

Kling[4] is of the opinion that the computer is an instrument of bureaucratic politics. He conducted a survey amongst managers, data analysts and clerks who make use of computers on a regular basis. At the lower levels of management it was maintained by those interviewed that there was an increase in the ease with which they could obtain the information needed to perform their tasks whilst higher levels of management maintained that they were able to ask for more complex analyses of data to be carried out and hence obtain more meaningful information from the computer system. People outside the context of line management argued that the computer appeared to have little utility so far as they were concerned.

Buro[4] maintains that the bulk of computing activity in most organizations is devoted to the support of routine operations such as transaction processing, record keeping and elementary financial transactions. He found that few resources were devoted to support managers in scheduling and allocation of resources and control of usage. Danz[4] claims that computers appear rarely to be used to support long-range planning and policy analysis.

## 6. Computers and Contracts

There is evidence that lack of experience at management level in the procurement of computers leads to difficulties. A common problem exists in otherwise disparate fields of activity. The problem is of two forms; one is where there is an ill-defined 'three-cornered' contractual arrangement between, typically, a hardware manufacturer, a software house and the intending end-user. The other is where no formal contract is in existence between any parties to cover the computer, the software and the job they are supposed to do. These situations arise when the prospective end-user asks, say, a vendor of software to design, for example, a stock-control system. After a brief analysis of the prospective end-user's working environment, the vendor will propose (for reasons of economy) the use of an already developed software unit (package) but with modifications particular to that end-user. The vendor will say that the package is designed to run on a particular hardware configuration manufactured by a particular computer manu-facturer. At that stage, however, the vendor will merely advise the end-user to buy the computer from a hardware vendor so avoiding a direct link himself with the hardware. The end-user in good faith will buy the recommended hardware and install it on his premises often untested and certainly ahead of the software which he then awaits. The software eventually is delivered but whilst satisfactory up to a point cannot perform

all the desired functions because of hitherto un-appreciated incompatibility with the hardware. The end-user has, however, by this time reor-ganized his business under the impression that changeover from a manual system to a computer system is both quick and easy.

The successful implementation of one company's software on another company's hardware and with no effective means of bringing the other two parties together is a recipe for disaster. Non-trivial sums of money are expended in this kind of process both in actual cash expenditure and in loss of revenue arising from the non-functioning computer system. In some cases organizations have been driven to the point of bankruptcy. Much of this could be avoided if attention is paid at the due time to proper forms of contract[5] between all parties which define responsibilities and possibly, penalty clauses, for late deliveries and implementation.

Everyone now runs some degree of risk as cheap computing spreads. At one time senior manage-ment would always be involved in the procurement of computers because they were expensive capital items. Management therefore had the opportunity of ensuring that when computer systems were installed they were adequately specified beforehand and tested before acceptance and payment. However, now, because of the cheapness of computers both in absolute and relative terms the procurement approval process has moved pro-gressively lower down the organizational structure and senior management may be rarely involved. This is, in corporate terms, strategically dangerous for the possible problems of computer usage without proper planning are not diminished just because a given computer is physically small and cheap. In some cases, the fact that the computer might be an inadequately-sized micro-computer can cause just as much if not more trouble than an over-loaded mainframe computer; the effects on the organization can, in local terms, be disastrous, unless planning is thorough and all concerned appreciate the strengths and weaknesses of computerized systems in all their possible forms.

## 7. Examples in British Industry

It is not easy to determine to what extent British Industry as a whole has understood the need for management of information as a corporate resource. If the number of published papers is taken as a guide a reasonable conclusion to draw would be that very few companies have, in fact, appreciated or understood the effect of the computer on information flow and still fewer have learned how to make full or better use of computers.

The theme developed so far in the paper is that broadly two criteria have to be met before change can occur; one is that senior management has to be aware of the need for change; the second is that the awareness must be translated into executive action resulting in reorganization. A necessary, prior, catalyst is the frame of mind of people at corporate level: reletive performance (however measured) is likely to be adversely affected when compared with competitors' performances. Examples of achievements in three disparate sections of U.K. industry shed a useful and instructive light on what can be achieved when senior management is aware of the need for information to be regarded as a corporate resource in competitive environments.

Before considering each of the three examples it is of interest to note that whilst, as mentioned above, the three organizations are from widely different sectors, they have one feature in common—each has a separate division or organization formed to provide a corporate (computer) systems service to groups, divisions or associated companies as appropriate. In at least one case (BL Systems Ltd) developed systems are sold as a commercial product to industry as a whole.

The point has already been made that the introduction of information handling systems of any significance must be planned in great detail. This is particularly true of distributed or multi-intelligence systems. The exact balance between on-line and off-line usage must be determined whilst allowance must be made for an increase in one relative to the other with time. For example it is well known that the actual use of visual display units with keyboards can rapidly exceed the planned use as people at different working levels begin to understand their advantages and so make increased demands on the system. Thus a check list of critical factors is a necessary starting point in design; examples of suitable criteria are—desired response time at terminals, simplicity of use by all personnel, timeliness and accuracy of data, expandability and ability of the system to function in case of partial failure, security of processing.

To return now to the examples, the first concerns a subsidiary company of Tube Investments[6] which had a particular business problem—to provide buyers with sufficient information to enable them to maximize their purchasing efficiency and keep control of goods received against orders placed. Approximately four hundred different types of purchased item are delivered daily.

The company has several years' experience of the use of computers for the provision of financial management information, and decided at the planning stage that a 'data base' approach should be used. This would avoid the problems caused by the same data being maintained on different systems many of which did not trap data movements at source.

The system finally adopted is based on a central large-scale (main frame) computer with one other computer and a number of terminals each geographically situated near the centre of activity with which it is concerned. The parts are connected by a network.

Broadly four different facilities are offered namely (i) data entry (of a non-real time nature) which forms approximately 20 per cent of transactions, (ii) real-time updating of data from vdus which forms about 25 per cent of transactions, (iii) simple enquiries (for example relationship between supplier code, order record, order number and delivery record) representing some 45 per cent of transactions, (iv) complex enquiries of an *ad hoc* nature which make use of complex data relationships; these represent about 10 per cent of transactions.

After 3 years of use the conclusion drawn by the company is that whilst no pretence is made that all the problems associated with the design and implementation of data bases and networking have been solved, the users at the different managerial levels have obtained significant benefits.

Willis, Faber and Dumas Ltd[7] is a firm of insurance brokers and underwriters. They function in a business environment typified by a vast amount of data recorded on paper. The increasing complexity of industrial life is directly reflected in increasingly sophisticated insurance requirements. Thus whilst computers have been used for many years for the processing of data, the need was to use them for text processing handling for example insurance slips, letters, reports, schedules, cover notes and policies all of which were being produced manually, iteratively—and expensively. In 1977 the decision was made to adopt computer-based text processing. Currrently Willis has two major installations (Ipswich and London) with over 50 vdus and 18 printers. Production of a wide variety of documents is computerized with each installation assessed in cost-effective terms.

The systems can communicate with each other and with a central main-frame. As a result documents are transferred 'in seconds' between London and Ipswich. The facility can be extended to a photo composer at the printing works. Documents can now be created for printing without additional art-work stages.

The conclusion drawn by the management of Willis, Faber and Dumas is that apart from the direct financial benefits and a better service to clients, improved presentation is possible together with greater accuracy, timeliness and flexibility—all highly important in a competitive environment.

As has been mentioned already, BL Systems Ltd not only develops systems for use throughout BL but also markets developed products. The third example is one of these—'See Why'[8] which is an interactive modelling system designed specifically for visual presentation of data and information. Unlike the other two examples it is based on the extensive use of micro-computer techniques. The system is designed to serve factory management by replacing large volumes of printout by a dynamic visual display in colour of any desired factory process. The manager can interact with the display, try out changes to, for example, production schedules, line layouts and simulation of equipment failures. He can also speed up simulation compressing the time, for example of a week's production run into a few minutes so enabling the effect of changed control rules to be assessed relatively quickly.

Applications of 'See Why' within BL[9] are those used in planning the Metro facilities. These cover five stages: (i) the total facility model as as aid to strategic decision-making; (ii) body-in white store which enables maximization of paint batch size; (iii) painted body store which enables the required throughout to be achieved by determination of control rules; (iv) line balancing which matches varying sales requirements and line sequencing constraints against the limits of the painted body store; (v) bolt-on items which enable alternative methods of manufacturing and transporting such items as doors.

## 8. Computers and Data Protection

The topics are well covered in the literature; one of the best sources in its day was the 'Report of the Committee on Data Protection'.[10] The author here presents a particular aspect of the problem with the express purposes of showing the role of security in an information context. Originally, when the term 'privacy' was used paradoxes arose when attempting to define privacy. Privacy and security were often taken to be synonymous. However, just as data and information were shown in Section 2 to differ from each other, so do privacy and security, a distinction still worth examining. It will help to understand the difference by describing a fictitious though by no means unlikely set of circumstances. We start by considering a vendor whose business is the selling of information. Nowadays he would be termed a 'data user'. As 'raw material' he acquires, legitimately, data from a variety of sources, for example address lists, results of surveys, the business trading records of various companies (receivers regard data as an asset to be sold as such). In each individual context the data may well be innocuous. It may consist of a mass of documents which need extensive sorting and perusal by human beings before anything of value in an information sense is available. Thus other than sorting for a given purpose would be impracticable due to the sheer magnitude of the task and the associated cost. However, in the context of computing (and making a reasonable assumption that the various

data sources will be in compatible form) the volume of data is of little consequence—a computer can sort the data, merge data items and search, speculatively, for correlation between data items. By this means new items of data can be produced which could have increased value (and hence become more marketable items) than the original data sets acquired by the vendor.

One such data user may own his own computer system, and employ his own support staff. Another may use the services of a commercial computer bureau with whom he will have a contract for the processing of, say, his magnetic tapes containing his data. In the case of both the pre-processed data has an initial value based largely on the cost of acquisition. After processing, when the new data may well be the highly marketable commodity the vendors desire, it becomes a valuable asset and needs protection. As such the level of protection will be appropriate to the value placed on it by the data user. The principle importance of the information to be gleaned from the new data items, however, is its timely use for the given purpose, so the protection has to be afforded until the data user judges the time is right to make use of the information. Both data users will therefore seek a degree of security appropriate to their particular method of working. For example the one with his own installation will ensure that the computer itself is housed in a secure environment and that his staff are appropriately selected and trained. The other, who uses a bureau service, will pay the bureau for the degree of security required during the processing and post-processing stages. He will also arrange to have the output of his processed data held under secure conditions at, say, his own premises.

These requirements for security are typical of perfectly proper and professionally run data processing activities. They are employed at many computer installations for entirely legal and laudable purposes and are as socially acceptable as, say, the security features used by banks. However, a different and sinister connotation results simply by implying that personal data is being processed and, by the use of the correlation sorting and merging techniques already mentioned, identifying particular individuals (data subjects, to use the correct term) and their likes, dislikes, habits and private activities. The data processing activity would take place under the secure conditions described thus giving rise to a paradox—security measures are aiding the potential invasion of privacy of individuals. Under the provisions of the draft Data Protection Bill now before Parliament, this may well be an offence. By implication the above has explained 'security' but it is more difficult to explain privacy, which is one reason why the emphasis has shifted to 'data protection'. One of the first mentions of privacy as the term is now understood is in article 12 of the United Nations Declaration of Human Rights. However, the declaration, whilst guaranteeing privacy, does not define it. The word privacy in fact means different things to different people; an example is 'credit'. One person (a potential data subject) may like to live entirely on credit and be largely insensitive to the requirement that as much of his personal financial data as is necessary to acquire a credit status be made available to a third party.

Another individual who regards the credit card system as anathema may be highly apprehensive about any process making available his personal financial data to a third party without his consent. Thus whilst the man who likes credit cards would regard constraints on movement of his personal data as a restriction on (if not an invasion of) his privacy, the anti-credit man would take precisely the opposite view.

Apart from personal financial data for credit purposes, there are other categories of data of a potentially sensitive nature—medical, habits, hobbies, family connections, social service record, career assessment, and in certain circumstances address and telephone numbers; the list is not exhaustive. Whilst the man who likes credit will be insensitive so far as availability of his personal financial data is concerned he may take great exception to a computing process which, by analysing his financial data in a certain way, detects that he spends numerous week-ends at Brighton. Clearly there are degrees of sensitivity. A person will expect different degrees of protection (security) to be applied by third parties who may be legitimate custodian and handlers of his personal data. He will then instinctively feel that his privacy is protected whereas the reality is that it may well not be. That, therefore, is a dilemma.

The motives for 'invasions of privacy' need not concern us in this paper. We need only note that the successful invasion of an individual's privacy by a third party could result in that individual having to do something he might not otherwise have done or, conversely, having to stop doing something he might otherwise have done. This summarizes the threat to society in the context of computers, information and privacy—the threat is made more real by the fact that a secure environment makes it easier to do and therefore more effective.

## 9. Computers and Crime

Computer fraud and computer crime are terms which appear with increasing frequency in the mass media; a recent novel uses computer fraud, plausibly, as a theme.[11] The impression is given throughout the media that such crime is widespread. In fact most of the serious analyses show that whilst computer crime is not as widespread as the media maintains or indeed as other crimes such as manual theft and fraud, crimes that have been committed by people using a computer have been highly successful in that large sums of money have been involved. What makes computer crimes of interest is the manner in which security systems are breached,[12] and the undoubted intelligent application of skill and clever manipulation of data by the criminals.

However, there is increasing evidence that not all computer crimes need this level of intelligence or professional skills to be held by the potential criminal. The evidence[13] shows that there is an increasing occurrence of crime where successful penetration has been accomplished by people who are barely literate but have an innate appreciation of the ways that computer systems can be breached. The reader who wishes to make a more detailed study of the misuse of computers is referred to other sources.[14]

Fraud can be defined as the theft of assets by intent; embezzlement as theft by someone in possession of a trust. To carry out these acts by means of a computer requires certain specific acts to be performed usually aimed at changing data in the computer system. Whilst altering data is easy, it is more difficult to conceal the fact that an alteration has been made without elaborate steps being taken to conceal the act—computers are therefore amenable to procedural control.

In most organizations where money-based transactions take place the accounting and auditing procedures which have been developed over the years ensure that a minimum of two people are involved in, for example the signing of cheques. This precaution is taken not because there is an inherent distrust of all the personnel involved but that it is common sense to have two people authorising payment so that the possibilities of illegal acts are made that more difficult; in the simple case of cheques the minimum would be the direct collusion of the two people who authorize the cheques. Unfortunately, when computer systems were first introduced on a wide scale in business many of these historical safeguards were totally ignored and one programmer would frequently be solely responsible for the accounting system. The fact that so few computer crimes have taken place is a testimony to the basic integrity and honesty of most computer people. However, there is no doubt that such defects in managerial control have allowed and still do allow crimes to be committed.

As knowledge of computer systems and potential areas of abuse has grown the established professions of accountancy and auditing have developed techniques to limit potential abuse. For some time now it has been good practise to 'design in' an audit trail, the word 'audit' having a more technical connotation than when used purely in an accounting context. The fact is that data can easily be changed, but that audit trails to detect such changes can be incorporated in a system (provided there is managerial awareness and a determination to act. Broadly, it is the reluctance or inability on the part of management to recognize these needs which present opportunities for computer misuse.

It is a common misconception that to commit a computer crime the potential criminal has to work in a 'Computer Centre' or for the organization owning the computer. He may, in fact, be so employed but does not have to be for the simple reason that most computer systems now have terminals attached which are geographically remote; the potential criminal can therefore be physically many miles away from the computer and have access to it over, say, telephone lines, and have no personal connection with either the computer or the organization owning the computer. What he does possess though is the vital information on how to penetrate the system. From then on the process can be compared with that between two game players where each watches for moves on the other's part and takes appropriate counter-moves.

Computer systems are vulnerable when the data contained in them becomes of sufficient value for it to be worth the time and effort of a third party to try to obtain illegal access, thereby extracting the necessary data. However, most computer systems cannot be made secure in a manner equivalent to the vaults of a bank because of the need, already mentioned, for continuous access from remote terminals.

Computers themselves are incapable of committing a fraudulent act (although they can make mistakes). Human beings are always involved, hence the people associated with computer systems should be selected carefully. The higher the value of the activity, the more diligent should be the selection mechanism. All this of course costs money and the provision and need for this has to be recognized by senior management. A number of questions can be posed by management to help the degree of risk to be assessed:

> Can computer files and programs (and the related operating and financial data) be modified by unauthorized personnel?
>
> Is a periodic independent computer audit performed regularly?
>
> Would damage to the computer system or loss of computer files cause substantial losses to the organization?
>
> What is the cost of re-creating computer files?

These questions are rarely asked and so rarely is the need for a policy understood.

As mentioned above comprehensive computer auditing is difficult unless the facilities for audit have been incorporated in the design stage of the system. The growth in data communications and transboarder data flow make the situation a great deal worse and legally complicated. There is at the time of writing no comprehensive U.K. legal code for movement of data let alone for the international aspects of data flow. As a result in the U.K. it has been necessary to rely on possible developments in case law. As was suggested in the DPC Report,[10] the enforcement of codes of practice could have been the first step in statute law. Pending the arrival of the Data Protection Act at present the only relevant offences under the U.K. criminal law appear to be, according to Devlin:[5]

(1) Conspiracy to defraud, etc.

(2) Offences under the Theft Act (1968).

(3) Criminal damage.

The law therefore at present appears to be an inadequate deterrent: offences cannot be defined precisely and associated legal costs are likely to be both lengthy and costly.

## 10. Conclusion

Adrian Norman[16] some time ago argued that the future of the U.K. Information Society needs to be debated just as once Imperial Preference, Free Trade and the Corn Laws were once debated. London has become the Insurance centre of the Western world, a status achieved by the concentration of expertise. It is possible that in a similar fashion the United Kingdom could become an information processor and husbander to the world and in doing so earn significant national income from the add-on value to the information processing. Information is not only a personal and corporate asset, it is a national asset and should be managed as such.

*References*

(1) T. R. H. Sizer, The hidden cost of minis, *Computer Weekly*, 29 November (1979).

(2) K. M. Sullivan, Does distributed processing pay off? *Datamation*, September (1980).

(3) S. Beer, Brain of the firm, Alen Lane (1972).

(4) K. Laudon *et al.*, *Computing Surveys*, Vol. 12, No. 1, March (1980).

(5) C. Tapper, *Computer Law*, Longman (1982).

(6) J. E. Austin, *A Practical Example of Combining a Central Data Base with Distributed Processing*, April (1978).

(7) A. J. Panham, Word processing in a word bound industry, *Policy*, September (1979).

(8) E. Fiddy, Seeing the model way to steer car assembly, *Computing*, 17 April (1980).

(9) R. B. Beadle, Private communication to the author, April (1981).

(10) HMSO, Report of the Data Protection Committee, December (1978).

(11)  J. McNeil, *The Consultant*, Weidenfeld and Nicolson (1978).

(12)  T. R. H. Sizer, Computer fraud, *Information Privacy*, Vol. 2, No. 6, November (1980).

(13)  M. Comer, *Computer Crime*, NCC Conference, London, July (1981).

(14)  M. Comer, *Computer Risk Management. Risk and Loss Control*, Autumn (1982).

(15)  K. Devlin, The legal aspects of computer systems, Conference on computerized information processing, London (1974).

(16)  A. R. D. Norman, Information farming, *Information Age*, Vol. 1, No. 4, March (1979).

# A Management Strategy for Information Processing

*A. C. Collins, Director of Corporate Planning and Managing Services, South Eastern Gas*

*This is the second of three articles on Management Strategy for Information Processing by this author. This paper discusses the methodology known as Business Systems Planning for assessing future computer systems requirements.*

## 1. Introduction

In late 1978 and through 1979 Segas undertook a two-phased study of their future computer systems requirements using the IBM methodology known as Business Systems Planning.

It was towards the end of 1978 that we decided, in Management Services, that a major review of our forward direction was appropriate after 3 years of intensive conversion and clearing up. It was also during the period of 1976 to 1978 that the first major elements of software required for the forward drive in mainframe systems was established. A major step was the conversion of the CRESSY system to operate under IBM's TP software, CICS.

During 1979 the second phase of the BSP was completed, logical data analysis and techniques were introduced and a data base team was established. The major development of new systems was continued using the systems priorities established during Phase I and II of the BSP process. A hierarchy of modelling was established, criteria for selecting W.P. equipment in-line with the Segas philosophy were established and the major programme of education was continued. This then is the background against which the Business System Planning study was undertaken.

Traditionally, systems have been developed along functional lines, that is to say, a system serving customer service was developed within the functional boundary of customer service. Where cross functional links were required, these were obtained by 'stitching across' from two systems not necessarily originally designed to interface. The primary emphasis of the systems was on the transactions carried out by clerks with fairly limited Management Information Systems derived from the transactions. Organizational structures and procedures strongly influenced the systems, thus providing the major barrier to transportability of systems. Data was not viewed as a corporate resource but as belonging to the function that 'owned' the system. Hence, it was possible for two systems with customer records to have separate files with cumbersome cross linking and updating, if indeed such updating existed at all.

I am sure this picture can be well recognized, and indeed, probably many of us still have some systems which confirm to this pattern. It will be some years in Segas before we have worked our way through a programme of replacing all systems of this type with cross-functional developments based upon our findings from Phase II BSP.

During 1978, after many discussions in Management Services, as to how we might establish a new basis for our forward system strategy, we became aware of the methodology developed by IBM, known as Business Systems Planning.

## 2. The Background to Business Systems Planning (BSP)

During the late 1960s and early 1970s, IBM in common with many other large organizations, found that their previous methodologies for planning information systems were inadequate. After much internal experimentation, distilling and refining, they developed the methodology of BSP for

The author is Director of Corporate Planning and Management Services for South Eastern Gas, Segas House, Katherine Street, Croydon CR9 1JU, U.K.

their own use and then introduced it as a consultancy service to their larger customers. By the mid-1970s it had been used by several hundred large IBM customers and some variations of it have been used by some of the management consulting companies, who address top management.

It is essentially a structured and formalized approach, to assist any business in establishing an Information Systems Plan, to satisfy its short and longer term information requirements. One of its greatest benefits is that it is a top down, strategic approach, requiring both commitment and involvement of senior members of the organization. In some instances it has been most useful as a vehicle for communication with top management on the subject of information system strategy rather than as a planning tool for information systems.

One essential message that emerges during the process is that 'Information is a Corporate Resource' and should be planned on a company wide basis, regardless of the fact that the information may be used in a number of different computers and by a number of different departments.

In general if a company remains in the same business area, the information processes will to a large extent remain the same, even though the organization may change over time. The process of cross functional transactions are defined as a series of 'business processes', the definition of which is an element in Business Systems Planning. By examining the relationship between organization and business processes, one establishes a view of the information architecture. This information architecture can therefore, be designed to be more independent of the current organization, of the company. Naturally implementation of the architecture will reflect the current organization but the systems should prove to be more adaptable and less dependent upon organizational structure than those which have been developed hitherto.

Another feature of the BSP methodology is that it is essentially a Corporate Planning approach to information systems and uses established procedures, such as 'Gap Analysis'. That is to say that the degree of support to the business from existing information systems is identified. The desired situation is also identified and the difference establishes the need for development. Further methodological approaches identify the priorities for the various systems and by more detailed analytical approaches a detailed information system strategy can be developed.

## 3. Objectives of Business Systems Planning

The overall objective of business systems planning is to ensure that the business has an Information Systems Plan that supports its short and long term information needs and is an integral part of the business plan. The following subsidiary objectives can be defined:

(1) To provide a formal, objective method to establish priorities for their information systems without regard to parochial interests.

(2) To ensure that systems are developed with a long life, thus protecting the systems investment. This is achieved by basing systems upon 'Business Processes', that are generally less affected by organizational change.

(3) To ensure that the data processing resources are managed in order to produce the most efficient and effective support of the business goals.

(4) To increase the confidence of management that higher return, major information systems will be produced.

(5) To improve the relationships between Computer Services department and end users where required, by providing for systems that are responsive to user requirements and user priorities.

(6) To ensure that data is considered as a corporate resource that should be planned, managed and controlled in order to be used effectively by the organization.

## 4. Benefits of Business Systems Planning

IBM have identified a number of benefits which BSP offers to top management, to functional and operational management, and to Computer Services Management.

(1) *Top Management*

(a) It provides an evaluation of how effective the current computer systems are supporting the business.

(b) It provides a defined, logical approach to assist in solving management control problems from a business perspective.

(c) It provides a means for assessing the requirements for future computer systems, using a methodology based on business related impacts and priorities.

(d) By applying a planned approach, it allows an early return on the organizations information systems investment.

(e) It provides a potential route for the development of computer based systems that are relatively independent of organizational structure.

(f) It provides confidence that the computer

systems direction is correct and that adequate management attention exists to implement the proposed systems.

(2) *To Functional and Operational Management*

(a) It provides a logical and defined approach, which assists in solving management control and operational control problems.

(b) It ensures that data is consistent and can be used and shared by all users having a requirement to do so.

(c) It ensures that functional management are involved, to establish organizational objectives and direction as well as agreed upon system priorities.

(d) It ensures that systems are management and user oriented, rather than data processing oriented.

(3) *To Computer Services Management*

(a) It provides a mechanism for communication with top management and ensures that top management are aware of the organization's information requirements.

(b) It provides agreed-upon system priorities.

(c) It can provide a better long range planning base for data processing resources and for funding.

(d) It ensures that Computer Services personnel are better trained and more experienced in planning data processing to respond to business needs.

# 5. Advantages of Business Systems Planning to IBM

Clearly there are a number of advantages in a customer of IBM undertaking such a study and IBM are not altruistic in providing this consultancy service. Certainly it can be a great aid to their customer but it also provides IBM with a first class opportunity for understanding the customer's business more clearly and thus being able to market to them with greater force. Since the whole approach involves senior management in the organization, it also provides IBM with the opportunity of establishing new contacts and developing direct relationships with functional users.

The identification of information as a corporate resource, is a message familiar to all of us. There is, as a consequence, a pressure to move towards data base techniques. Indeed a high proportion of the customers who have undertaken BSP, have as a consequence moved to data base using IMS. Segas

after completing Phase II of BSP, decided to use DL/1, the IBM data base language, after evaluating the merits of some eight different DBMS packages.

# 6. The BSP Methodology

The BSP process consists of two separate stages:

*Phase I*
This is a top-down strategic level study of the business and its environment, relating the current information systems support given to key decision areas. It identifies not only the strengths and weaknesses of existing systems, but also the additional systems required and their priorities.

*Phase II*
This is a more detailed in depth study which takes a somewhat larger team a longer period of time. The primary objectives of this Phase is to establish the data relationships required for introduction of database techniques, to establish a data dictionary, and to prepare an overall Information Systems Plan in detail and to specify the resource requirements to achieve the plan.

The Two Phased approach provides a break point at the end of Phase I where the client(s) are able to review the progress of the study. Both Phases I and II are undertaken by a Task Force approach. That is to say a dedicated team carries out the exercise with clearly defined objectives and over a specified period of time.

As a general rule IBM will not undertake a study of BSP with a client's company unless it has the full support of the Chief Executive of the company. It is essential that he is committed to the study and is prepared to act on the findings of the Task Force. In Segas the Chairman of the Region commissioned the study after a presentation on the subject and having had a verbal report from several other major companies who had carried out similar studies. The client group was the Chairman and Executive Committee of the Region who in effect acted as the Steering Group for the project both in Phase I and Phase II.

The Phase I Task Force consisted of business managers who were at a sufficiently senior level of responsibility to be able to contribute effectively to a strategic overview. This was undertaken as a full time commitment lasting four weeks and was led by the Deputy Chairman of the Region. The team comprised:

Deputy Chairman (Task Force Co-ordinator)
Controller of Management Services
Personnel Manager
Regional Marketing Manager
Assistant Distribution Engineer
Financial Systems Manager
Computer Services Manager

In addition the Team was supported by a senior IBM consultant, the IBM Accounts Manager to Segas and a systems engineer. It can therefore be seen that there was a considerable investment of effort from senior managers to the exercise, emphasizing the importance that the Region attributed to it.

The objectives of the Phase I Study were:

(1) To strengthen an overall understanding of the business in which Segas is involved.

(2) To assess the current level of support given to the business processes by the existing Information Systems.

(3) To understand the functional relationships and information needs of management.

(4) To recommend the first area of development with a general estimate of its value.

(5) To recommend an action plan for preparing for, and conducting Phase II of the Study if required.

An important part of the BSP methodology is the recognition that there are four elements which influence information processes, namely, organizational structure, 'business processes', data and the information systems. These four elements are sometimes referred to as the 'Iron Cross' and are illustrated in Figure 1. Some explanation is required of what a 'business process' is.

A business process is defined as an essential decision or activity required to manage and/or administer the resources and operations of the company. One such process was defined as 'Manage Cash'. Each business process has a life cycle associated with it, covering planning, initiating the process, maintaining the process, and completing the cycle. The subsidiary elements defined for 'Managing cash' are illustrated in Figure 2. A similar analysis for 'Managing New Industrial Commercial and New Housing Gas Sales', is illustrated in Figure 3. In all 13 essential business processes were defined to cover the entire operations of Segas.

---

1. **Forecast the Cash Flow**

   Consolidate Revenue and Capital Budgets and Forecast Receipts and Payments

2. **Generate the Cash Flow Inwards**

   Read Meters, Clear Prepaid Meters, Bill for Gas, Appliances and Fitting Work

3. **Control Payments**

   Authorise Expenditure and Control Payments for Goods and Services Received and Administer the Payroll

4. **Monitor Performance**

   Reconcile Banking, Compare Actual Cash Flow With Forecast, Compare Actual Income and Expenditure With Budget and Take/Recommend Any Necessary Corrective Action

Figure 2. Managing cash

---

1. **Survey and Evaluate Market Potential**

   Carry Out Commercial and Industrial Energy User Surveys; Measure Fuel Usage Other than Gas and Assess the Proportion that Could be Converted to Gas Use, Taking into Account Pricing and Other Economic Factors, Technical Aspects, etc.

   Examine Planning Applications for Housing Development and Assess the Prospects of Getting Gas Laid on Economically

2. **Establish Targets**

   Taking the Assessment of Potential, Set Targets for Capturing the Possible New Business Year by Year. Agree Targets with B.G. H.Q.

3. **Plan Operations**

   Assess Resources — Primarily Manpower — Needed to Achieve Sales Targets. Formulate Action Plans for Customer Contact and Selling

4. **Manage Sales Force**

   Direct the Sales Force Day to Day to Achieve Action Plan and, Consequently Sales Targets

5. **Monitor Performance**

   Regularly Monitor the Achievement of Sales Against Targets to Assess Progress

Figure 3. Managing new industrial commercial and new housing gas sales

---

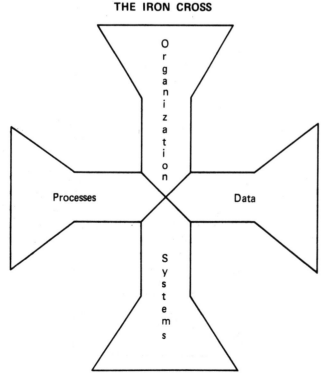

THE IRON CROSS

Organization

Processes    Data

Systems

Figure 1. Overall information system plan

The primary mission of Segas was defined as 'to supply a gas energy service', which was explained as 'To supply customers with an adequate gas energy service, safely and meet industry objectives and targets consistent with government established policy'. The 13 subsidiary business processes were seen as enabling the organization to achieve this mission.

The process steps of the Phase I BSP are shown in Figure 4, but the process can be divided into four tasks namely:

(1) Analysing the Segas business environment and specifying objectives for each department.

(2) Identifying business processes and data classes which support the business.

(3) Interviewing senior managers in the organization, to verify the Task Force's perception of Segas and to identify the priorities of senior management in the organization for new systems development.

(4) Synthesizing from the analysis and interviews a set of strategic priorities for future action. At the conclusion the Task Force reports back to the sponsor(s).

The relationships between the four elements of the Iron Cross are expressed in the form of a series of matrices, each involving two of the parameters. Then by over-laying the matrices created, a picture of the support from current information systems of the key business processes and decisions are produced.

The heart of any BSP Study consists of the interviews with senior managers. The Managers interviewed will normally be no more than two levels below the Chief Executive of the company. They should be responsible for major functions such as Finance, Engineering, Personnel, Marketing etc.

In Segas, 13 interviews were conducted including the Chairman, the Executive Committee, several Chief Officers and representatives of functional area and district management.

The purpose of the interviews were:

(1) To validate the matrices and data collected.

(2) To determine the information needed by executives and to place a value on it.

(3) To place priorities on the need for future applications.

(4) To determine the current problems.

(5) To gain executive rapport and involvement.

The interview procedure was a formal process involving the Task Force Co-ordinator and several observers who took structured and unstructured notes of the interview. The matrices derived were shown as wall charts and each interviewee was asked to validate them at the start of the interview. In particular the list and description of business processes was agreed to or modified.

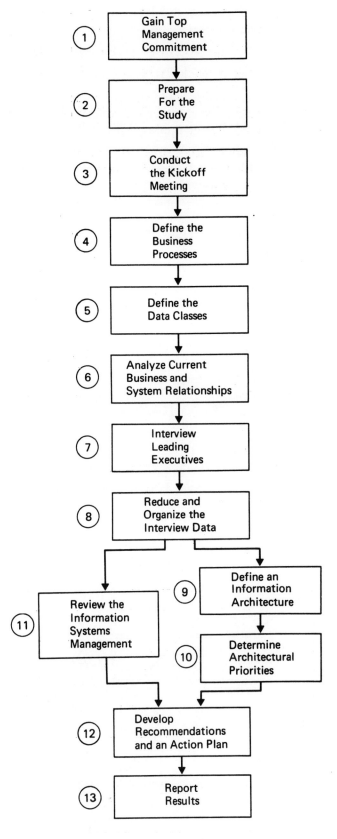

Figure 4. The steps in a BSP study

Some of the questions which were asked during the interviews were:

(1) What are your specific responsibilities? Are they different from those indicated on the organization chart?

(2) What are the basic objectives of your function?

(3) What are the three greatest problems you have had in meeting these objectives? (Not only current problems but problems of the recent past also.)

(4) What has prevented you solving them?

(5) What is needed to solve them?

(6) What value would better information have in these areas (in person hours saved, pounds saved, better opportunities etc)?

(7) In what other areas could the greatest improvements be realized, given better information support?

(8) What would be the values of these improvements?

(9) What costs may be incurred by inaccurate or untimely information?

(10) What is the most useful information you receive? (The best aspects of current systems must be retained.)

(11) What would you most like to receive?

(12) How would you rate your current information support with respect to:
   (i) Types of information
   (ii) Timeliness
   (iii) Accuracy
   (iv) Adequacy
   (v) Cost
   (vi) Consistency
   (vii) Ease of use or clarity of presentation?

(13) How are you measured by your superior?

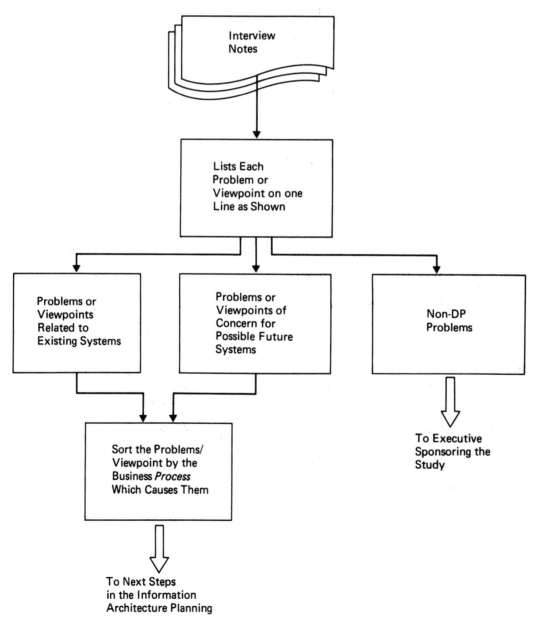

Figure 5. Consolidation of the data from executive interviews

(14) How do you measure your subordinates?

(15) What other kinds of measurement are you expected to make?

(16) What kinds of decisions are you expected to make? What computer aids might help you in your decision making?

(17) What major changes are expected in your area in the next year? Over the next 2, 4 or 6 years?

(18) What do you expect and what would you like the result from this study?

(19) Any additional views or comments?

In a number of cases the viewpoints expressed are perceived problems which may or may not be real problems. Perceived problems are traced back to root causes and forward to quantifiable effects if possible. Each interviewee was given a summary of the interview and asked to confirm that it was correctly recorded and understood. The problems/viewpoints were divided into three categories:

(a) Not related to computer services or information systems.

(b) Problems which are related to current information systems.

(c) Problems related to possible future information systems.

Each problem or viewpoint recorded is summarized in a record which included the following elements:

(a) The problem statement.

(b) Potential solution.

(c) Value statement.

(d) Information system need.

(e) The business processes affected.

(f) The business process which caused the problem.

Figure 5 illustrates the condensation process used to reduce the interview to a set of problems and potential actions.

A number of new information systems can be identified from the matrices and the interviews with senior managers. Having identified these the team establishes a procedure to set development priorities, which involves three steps.

(1) The identification of dependency between the new systems required and existing systems.

(2) The valuation of new systems against a number of objective criteria used to select priorities.

(3) Categorizing systems into high, medium and low priorities resulting from the above evaluation

and into implementation time scale in the essential sequence imposed by the dependencies.

The criteria listed under (2), were classified as those of 'major significance', including return on investment, customer satisfaction and safety implications. A second category termed 'important' was the strength of user demand and a third category termed 'noteworthy', included whether the project was of high or low risk as a possibility of success.

At the end of the one month period the Task Force reported back to the Chairman and the Executive Committee. It has concluded that new systems or extensions of existing systems were required in 18 areas, (listed in Figure 6). It was also recommended

1. New Customer Gas Billing System
2. Contract Gas Sales
3. Prepayment Gas
4. Budget,Billing
5. Litigation System
6. Data Capture in Showroom
7. Market Research
8. Personnel Information for Line Managers
9. Test
10. Distribution Job Planning
11. Productivity of Workforce
12. Digitised Mapping
13. Self-Evaluating Track Sheets
14. Transmission Materials
15. Transmission Records
16. Integrated Supplies System
17. Creditor Payments
18. Control of Capital Expenditure

Figure 6. Proposed new systems

that Phase II of the study should proceed and that the team should consist of the Manager, Computer Services (Task Force Co-ordinator), the Database Manager and functional representatives. It was agreed that during Phase II the functional representatives would be involved full-time for approximately 12 weeks, in early 1979 and for 1 or 2 days per week for 6 months. In fact the time involvement was substantially less than this, although the elapsed time for Phase II, took overall approximately 1 year (see Figure 7).

The tests proposed for the Phase II Study, are outlined in Figure 8. It can be seen that the tests are

- Nine Months Full-Time for 3 of Computer Services Data Management Section

- Two Weeks Full-Time for All Members in July 1979 for Training and Briefing

- Four Weeks Part-Time for User Representatives During Analysis of Their Function

- Further Involvement at Final Stages to Agree Content and Write Report

Figure 7. Phase II study

1.  More Detailed Analysis of Business Processes
2.  Identify and Classify Data
3.  Analyse Problems and Propose Solutions
4.  List Benefits of New Systems
    — Quantified Where Possible
5.  Update List of Computer Systems
    — Recommend Allocation of D.P. Resources
6.  Formalise an Information Systems Plan
7.  Specify First New System in Some Detail
8.  Recommend Best Way to Manage Ongoing I.S.P.

Figure 8. Phase I—tasks for Phase II

at a lower level and involve analysis of data (using the LDA approach).

The major recommendations of the Phase II Study are outlined in Figure 9, where it can be seen that

- Establish Systems Management Group

- Establish 'Information Centre'

- Database Structuring of Major Data Areas

- Acquistion of D L/1

- N.I.A.S. Pilot Scheme

- Appoint Data Co-ordinators

Figure 9. Phase II—major recommendations

the major issues were to move to database using DL/1 as the database language and to use a front ending system to NIAS as the pilot scheme. It was also identified as essential to have data co-ordinators appointed in each function who would liaise with the Database Manager and Data Administrator within Computer Services.

# Managing the Growth of Electronic Office Information Systems

*R. A. Hirschheim, London School of Economics and Political Science*

*Organizations, and particularly their information services departments, are facing more difficult problems as society inexorably moves into the information age. The ability of organizations to survive in the future may very well depend upon their capacity to satisfactorily cope with the pace of technological change. With the rate at which technologies such as word processors, electronic mail, personal computing, facsimile devices, private automatic branch exchanges (PABXs), voice recognition systems, intelligent copiers, to name but a few, are being introduced in organizations, well thought out information management strategies are needed. The purpose of this paper is to propose a stage theory of growth which could help organizations develop appropriate information management strategies dealing with electronic office information systems;\* and additionally, to underline the key role that electronic information systems may play as organizations face the problems of moving into the information age.*

There appear to be three trends associated with the coming of the information age which will have a great bearing on the way organizations—particularly information services departments—operate.

## Trend One—The Pace of Information Technological Change

Numerous individuals have predicted the rate of information technological change will increase to the point where it will seem out of control. (Indeed, some people feel we have already arrived at this point.) Many organizations will be unable to cope with the pace of the information technological change and will fall further and further behind on the technological learning curve. Those organizations which can keep pace with the change will gain a competitive advantage. If this is true, then some means to accelerate the absorption of information technological change must be found as the alternative may be fewer and fewer organizations; that is, only those organizations who can successfully keep pace with the new technologies will survive. Electronic office information systems may provide a vehicle for satisfactorily dealing with information technological change in that they offer the possibility of gradual and evolutionary implementation of the technology. An organization could start off with stand alone word processors and personal computers and gradually add the links to intelligent copiers, high-speed printers, facsimile devices and other internal facilities, and also links to external facilities—value added networks, voice networks and the like. These links could take the form of local area networks—for internal facilities—and computerized branch exchanges or PABXs—for external facilities.

## Trend Two—The Pace of Organizational Environment Change

This trend is related to information technological change but is more pervasive; it is the pace of world-wide change and is exemplified by the writings of Alvin Toffler in *Future Shock* and *The Third Wave*. Basically, the trend suggests society is changing at an ever increasing rate. Things we have taken for granted for so long may no longer be true in the future. Who would have ever thought a major U.S. city such as New York could go bankrupt, yet it very nearly did. And Concorde, the marvel of its time, costs the British tax payer millions of pounds a year. It was conceived of and designed when fuel was inexpensive. The thought of quadrupled fuel prices never entered the experts' minds at the time.

The author is Lecturer in Systems Analysis at the London School of Economics and Political Science, Houghton Street, London WC2A 2AE.

\*Electronic office information systems go under many titles: office automation, the electronic office, the office of the future, office information systems, the paperless office, are but a few.

And so on. The point is, as the rate of change accelerates, an organization's environment becomes more unstable. With more instability and uncertainty an organization will need to process more information. (This is a key point made by Galbraith[1] in his seminal work on the information processing capabilities of organizations.) Thus, the demand on an organization's information services function to store, process, analyse and retrieve more information in an expeditious manner will increase. Further, areas which hitherto used little, if any, computer and computerized communication facilities may be forced—because of the environment—to implement computerized information systems. Electronic information systems appear particularly relevant here in that they provide a vehicle for processing information much more efficiently. Office workers have had few technologies over the past century which provide such a potential for improvement as the new technology. (Some statistics provided later in the paper underscore this point.) It is clear that one of the key features of electronic office information systems is the potential of the technology to dramatically improve an office worker's ability to process and communicate information.

## Trend Three—The Growth of Industrial Democracy

A third trend has to do with people and their desire to change society. Many authors have noted a growing trend in the west for people wanting more autonomous environments—both in respect to work and leisure. The argument asserts that individuals should have the right to participate or have some say in anything which affects them. This has variously been referred to as industrial democracy, worker participation, and so on.* Additionally, the trend sees individuals seeking more satisfying, less stressful, and more recognition enhancing jobs. Again, electronic office information systems can play a valuable role in satisfying these desires. The technology can lead to jobs which are much more exciting and rewarding. For example, the change from a typist to a word processing operator offers the person a job with greater status and makes the typing of a document much easier. It can enhance job satisfaction in that the word processing operator has the potential for greater interaction with the author of the document than existed in the typing pool days. Portable work stations provide the office worker with greater freedom in terms of when, where and how he does his work. He has the ability to work at home, in a hotel, in a different office, etc. by just tying in to the office system via a telecommunication or other data network link. The possibilities appear unlimited and have been well described in the literature.

On the other hand, the technology associated with electronic office automation systems can produce jobs which are potentially less satisfying, de-skilled and far more stressful. For example, the technology which permits more flexibility in work concomitantly permits a number of abuses. A manager who is interested in having more control over his employees has the capability through workstations. At any point in time he would have the ability to see exactly what an employee is, or is not doing. All he has to do is access his employee's workstation through his own and he will know precisely what the employee is doing. This could hardly be considered less stressful for the employee. Additionally, the potential for a 12–16 hour work day exists. An individual feeling the burden of not being able to finish his work at the office may be tempted to bring his terminal home with him to continue working. And although one may argue this is possible even without terminals and technology, i.e. bringing paperwork home, the potential for a 16 hour work day is greater with the new technology than without. The implications of the extended work day on family life, health—both physical and mental, and the like, clearly offers some cause for concern. The possibility for de-skilled jobs, due to new information technology, is also cause for concern. Numerous authors have, however, written extensively on this subject and it will, therefore, not be treated here.

In summary, electronic office information systems have the potential for enhancing organizational worker's jobs—both materially and mentally— thus leading to a better quality of working life for any office worker. They also have the potential to produce jobs which are de-skilled, repetitive, less interesting and more stressful. The choice, presumably, is in the hands of the organization;* if so, it should make the most of it.

## Other Reasons for the Growth of Interest in Electronic Office Information Systems

Besides the fact that certain trends in the coming information age lead to a promising future for electronic office information systems, other—more basic and oft-quoted—reasons exist. They are as follows:

### (1) The Productivity Argument
The argument is very basic. Over the past decade industrial productivity has risen almost 90 per cent

---

*This trend is very much reflected in the issues raised by the trade unions—particularly those in Europe. See Nygaard[2] for a good treatment on this subject.

*This is a very contentious point which, no doubt, warrants considerable treatment. Unfortunately, any such treatment would require a great deal of space. It must, therefore, be beyond the scope of this paper. For more information see reference 12.

while office productivity has managed only a 4 per cent increase. Operating costs in the office, over the same period, have nearly doubled. The result has been an increase in the overall proportion of total corporate costs attributed to the office from 20 to 30 per cent to the present 40–50 per cent.* Traditionally, corporations have made little capital investment in their office workers; estimates suggest the figure to be between $2000 and $6000 per office worker. By comparison, the average capital expenditure for the industrial (factory) worker is estimated to be about $25,000.

The conclusion, which may be drawn, is that the reason for such a low office productivity increase is the small capital expenditure per office worker. Thus, an increased capital expenditure in the office could lead to higher office productivity.

Although the conclusion may be right—and many people intuitively feel it is obvious—there are two possibilities which need to be considered. One, the assumption that higher capital expenditure leads to higher productivity in the factory may or may not be true. There have clearly been cases where the implementation of new machinery and technology has actually led to lower productivity, worker unrest, sabotage and the like. Similarly, in the cases where there was an increase in productivity, how much of it is actually due to the higher expectations placed on the workers by management? Or, perhaps the workers felt compelled to work harder because they feared for their jobs. The correlation between capital expenditure and productivity— although not spurious—may be much weaker than we think.

Two, comparing the productivity increases in office worker with factory workers and therefore concluding productivity in the office must increase, may be incongruous. That is, the relative starting points for comparison may be totally different. It is conceivable that 10 years ago, the factory worker was highly unproductive but through technology, better working methods and procedures, etc., it became possible to increase his productivity markedly. This may not be the case with the office worker. If 10 years ago he was reasonably efficient in his job, then it is understandable why his productivity has not risen greatly. There may be little scope for making his job more productive.

In summary, although the literature and systems vendors may present a compelling argument for asserting an increase in capital expenditure on the office worker will lead to dramatic increases in office productivity, this argument may not be as strong as they might suggest. However, this is not to say that the new technology will not lead to greater office productivity; rather, a more tempered expectation about electronic office information systems needs to be adopted.

(2) *The Growing Number of Office Workers Argument*
This argument suggests the need for office technology based on the sheer number of people involved in office and administrative jobs. The number of people who make their living in the office or office related jobs is rising every year. Zisman[3] reported that 22 per cent of the U.S. labour force was involved in office work. Other figures are more dramatic. Based on a 1981 U.K. Department of Employment study,* 7,791,400 British workers—34.2 per cent of the labour force—are engaged in office, professional and technical occupations (often referred to as the 'knowledge worker' occupations). In the U.S., the figure is even higher: 37,151,000 workers comprising 50 per cent of the labout force with a total wage bill of almost $600m per annum.†

There are two concerns surrounding the growth in office workers. One, as the numbers grow, a greater and greater proportion of total corporate costs will be based on office costs; the present figure seems to be between 40 and 50 per cent. And as salaries, the cost of materials, etc. rise, this figure will continue to increase. Two, it has been reported[4] that even with a high rate of unemployment in the U.K., there is still a shortage of skilled and experienced office staff. It is suggested this trend is likely to continue.

(3) *The Office Market Argument*
A third argument for the growth of office technology is related to all the others and might be considered self-fulfilling. That is, as the need for new electronic office information systems grows, the information technology industry will expand to meet this demand. As the industry grows it will, through advertising, publicity, etc., cause the demand for office technology to grow, and so on. This, it is expected, would have a spiralling effect.

Market forecasts for the office technology area vary substantially; but no matter what forecast is read, the expected expenditure is substantial. For example, *Business Week* in 1975 predicted the market for office systems technology would reach $85bn; in the U.S. by the middle-to-late 1980s. A Canadian Department of Communications study[5] predicted the Canadian market alone would be worth $10–15bn by the end of the 1980s. The study also expected the U.S. market to exceed $220bn by 1988.

There is little doubt that electronic office system technology will be big business. With giants of the

---

*These figures come from a study appearing in *Business Week*, June 30 (1975).

*New Earnings Survey, U.K. Department of Employment, February (1981).
†U.S. Employment and Earnings, U.S. Bureau of Labour Statistics, January (1981).

computer and communications industry such as IBM, AT&T and Xerox—not to mention Exxon's initiative—all vying for a part of the office market, the future promises to be an interesting one.

## Strategy Considerations for Electronic Office Information Systems

It is probably inevitable that electronic office information systems will become pervasive—particularly as the technology moves closer to handling all forms of voice, video and mixed-text input. As office technology evolves, the question facing organizations is 'what strategy should be adopted to accommodate the growth of office technology?' This, of course, is not easy to answer; it would depend on such considerations as: (1) the technology available today and what is expected in the future, (2) the predicted cost of the technology in the future, (3) the present and future needs of the organization, (4) the projected impact of the technology in terms of worker reaction, (5) the implications on staff numbers, i.e. redundancies, hiring new staff, etc., (6) the availability of qualified or suitable staff, (7) training—its costs and content, (8) the suitability of the physical structures, e.g. buildings, offices, etc., to the adoption of new technology, (9) the potential rearranging of the organization, i.e. its structure due to new technology, (10) the present and anticipated resources of the organization, and (11) the existing socio-political climate. This list is not exhaustive, rather it suggests the type of issues an organization must address if it is to develop an appropriate strategy for new office technology.

At present, there are few formalized strategy building frameworks upon which organizations can build electronic office systems strategies. This is partly because of the newness of the area—there has been little experience with new office technology—and partly because of the complexity of designing and then implementing an electronic office information systems strategy.

Some of the complexity in designing a strategy comes from the issues cited above. Yet, there is another more fundamental point, which is only peripherally touched on above—namely, the nature of office work. Office work is for the most part knowledge work. That is, the worker depends on his intelligence, perception, abilities and knowledge of the subject, to accomplish the tasks at hand. Various authors have attempted to describe and document the office worker and his environment.

Hammer and Sirbu,[6] in describing the research on office technology done at MIT, make three observations about offices. First, offices and their activities tend to be distributed both in space and time. They involve the continuous coordination of parallel activities in many locations. Second, office activities, although often routine are more often changing. The office worker must constantly revise his activities to cope with the dynamic environment of today's organizations. Third, rarely are problems solved except by the action of several persons in an interactive exchange of ideas and commitment. In fact, much of what transpires in an office is group work involving the simultaneous participation of several persons, rather than a sequence of activities performed by autonomous actors.

Ellis[7] and his group at Xerox PARC view offices from a slightly different perspective. They conceive of offices as complex, highly parallel, interactive information processing systems and have developed a formalism for dealing with the information flows in an office. Through interviews and observation they attempt to record office activities—which are based on information flows—by means of their developed formalism. The formalism describes office information flows in terms of procedures, activities, resources and precedence constraints. These are recorded in graphical form through the use of what is called information control nets. This approach yields a description of an office which may be useful in determining those office activities amenable to automation. Ellis claims that the information control net approach can also lead to the discovery of inefficient or inappropriate activities in an office which can then be rectified.

It has also been noted, that in general, the more senior an employee is, the more varied and unpredictable are his duties and tasks. Any attempt to automate or support these tasks through office technology becomes more difficult the higher up the organization one goes. Further, as Mintzberg[8] quite rightly shows, even the work of lower level managers is much more unstructured and varied than what conventional wisdom may suggest. Thus, any attempt to design an electronic office information systems strategy must recognize the highly varied and unstructured tasks performed by the knowledge worker in the office.

## Stages of Growth in Electronic Office Automation Systems

Richard Nolan and Cyrus Gibson[9] put forward a four stage theory of data processing growth in organizations. Later, Nolan[10] extended the four stages to six to include the growth of data administration and the concept of information resource management. The key aspect of the stage theory of growth, which reflects the classical S-shaped learning curve, is that organizations take time to learn about and adjust to computer-based systems. Additionally, these systems invariably change the way the organization operates.

Based on the Nolan/Gibson stage theory of data processing growth, Zisman[3] proposed one for office automation. It embraces the four stages of initiation, expansion, formalization and maturity as set out by Nolan and Gibson.[9] Zisman[3] sees initiation as the stage where organizations will perceive technological opportunities for cost reductions and increase productivity and will begin to implement some of the more rudimentary electronic office technologies such as text processors, telex and the like. Emphasis will be on the more efficient production of paper (as opposed to the long term objective of reduced paper work). The technology will normally be introduced and managed by the administrative services function.

Expansion, according to Zisman, will follow initiation, emphasizing the development of tools to mechanize the tasks that people perform, e.g. typing, filing, etc. However, this stage will not attempt to automate office functions nor show any great concern for the integration of these tools into a cohesive whole. Zisman feels the major obstacle to this stage will be the organization—particularly its people—rather than the technology.

The period of rapid expansion which follows initiation will see a proliferation of disjointed technological tools. This will give rise to the need for formalization and circumspection upon which a change in emphasis will occur. Part of this change will be a movement toward integrating applications and technologies into a cohesive whole. Another part of the change will cause a shift from mechanizing tools and tasks to automating processes and functions. This stage will finally start to address the problems faced by managers rather than only those of the secretary.

The fourth stage is that of maturity and ushers in a period of stabilization as the organization adapts to the changes brought about by office automation. There will be a continuation of integration in the office, and more office procedures will be automated as more is learned about them and the technology.

Zisman's view of the growth of office technology is a compelling one and very similar to our own. Based on the research into information management conducted at the London School of Economics, we note a growth in electronic office information systems which, in the main, mirrors Zisman's projections, although we see an additional dimension. The LSE research has used a longitudinal, case study approach—over a 3-year period—to determine and attempt to understand the nature of change in the information management policies or approaches adopted by information services departments across a spectrum of organizations in the U.K. Information management in this context is referred to as the:

'approach or policy adopted by an organization to manage its formal information resource. It embraces those formal information systems existing in an organization which provide information to organizational personnel, the information technology used to store, process retrieve, generate, etc., the information, and the implementation approach used to introduce new information systems and information technology in the organization.'

Since office technology is part of an organization's information technology, we were able to note many of the trends suggested by Zisman, although we refer to the stages somewhat differently and see an additional aspect or dimension not covered in Zismans' stage theory. We see the stages as follows:

*Stage One: Initiation*
This stage may also be seen as the stand-alone/activity-oriented stage. It is very similar to the one envisaged by Zisman. In this stage independent, stand-alone devices are bought as the potential for increased productivity and/or reduced costs is perceived. The most common technologies associated with this stage are word processors, personal computers, telex, etc. It is activity-oriented because technology is viewed in terms of enhancing a specific office activity, e.g. typing, calculating, filing etc. Organizations often see this as a time to 'experiment' with new technology.

*Stage Two: Contagion*
This stage may be seen as the cooperative/activity-oriented stage. Here office technology catches on and spreads quickly through the organization; Nolan[10] terms this 'superficial enthusiasm'. Users of the technology look for more cooperative ventures and find them in technologies such as electronic mail, shared databases, etc. It is still activity-oriented as the central focus is still on the activities of various office personnel. Similarly, organizations still view this time as one of experimentation and getting on the 'technological learning curve' so as not to be left behind.

*Stage Three: Control*
At some point in time, senior management will start to recognize the uncontrolled and widespread nature of office technology implementation and will want to get a handle on the growth. This may arise through a realization that the amount spent on office technology will have been rising at a very high rate—perhaps 30 per cent or more—per annum. Much of the growth in expenditure will come about not so much from the purchase of expensive pieces of equipment, rather from large quantities of relatively small amounts (less than £10,000) of various office technology, e.g. personal computers, work stations, graphics devices, and the like. Management, noting the uncoordinated and uncontrolled nature of the growth, will attempt to introduce control mechanisms to slow the growth and provide some breathing space while a satisfactory strategy is developed. This stage for all

intents and purposes, signifies the end of the time for experimenting with new office technology. It is a time for reflection and consolidation.

## Stage Four: Integration

This stage builds on the attempt for consolidation started in the previous stage. A firm strategy for the planned growth and development of office technology is worked out and implemented. Part of the strategy is the integration of the various pieces of office systems and technology already existing in the organization. The orientation of office technology changes as well during this stage. That is, there is a change in orientation from the activity-oriented approach—enhancing specific office activities—to a more process-oriented view. The process-oriented view focuses on office processes and functions, and is much more global in perspective. This view enables the development of true electronic office information systems to take place.

## Stage Five: Maturity

As organizations learn more about electronic office information systems, some new applications and uses of the technology will be thought of, but in general, this will mostly be a time for stabilization. Growth will slow down and there will be a continuing integration of functions and processes in the office. Concomitantly, there will be a final merging of the information technology and systems of the office with that of the rest of the organization. This will have been occurring—in some form or another, at a greater or lesser velocity—through most of the stages of growth, The final product will be some form of overall information resource function with an information resource management strategy.

Note, this growth theory of electronic office information systems is only an attempt at describing the stages an organization goes through in addressing office technology. The stages are described in rather broad terms because every organization will respond to office technology in a slightly different fashion. Yet the general thrust of these stages seems to have strong intuitive appeal and mirror the predictions of the so-called 'experts' of the field.

# Information Technology Approaches

One of the problems with a stage theory of electronic office information systems growth, is the assumption that an organization will embark on an office systems and technology introduction campaign which is—or must be—similar to all others. In the broadest of senses, this is probably true. There is a certain amount of learning which has to be done at each stage and there is no getting around that fact. However, as has been noted by

Hirschheim,[11] all organizations do not necessarily approach the issue of information technology introduction with the same 'frame of mind'. Hirschheim categorizes three types of organizational approaches to information technology.

(1) *The procrastinator.* This is the kind of organization which is extremely cautious and conservative. It is not willing to 'get burnt' on new technology so is quite prepared to wait and see what happens to other organizations. A common motto is we will 'wait until the technology is proven'. Of course this is a matter of judgment; for some, many years would be needed to prove the technology satisfactory. Another famous motto is 'technology is coming down in price, we are going to wait until it reaches bottom'. In fact, when the price does reach bottom it is probably because the technology is obsolete. Other arguments often used by the procrastinator are: 'we do not know enough about the technology so we need to research it in detail'; 'our manual system has worked well in the past and as our business grows we will just hire additional staff'; 'we cannot afford the new technology'; 'it is too complicated' and so on. Many of these organizations would like to be more adventuresome with new technology but they always manage to find excuses for why they should not.

(2) *The innovator.* This is the kind of organization who sees itself as an industry leader. Chances are they may have experimented with a number of new business techniques when they are first introduced, e.g. MBO, PPBS, ZBB, matrix management, etc. Information technology is no different. If it can help make the organization more productive, then it should be strongly considered. In these organizations, technology and industry leadership often go hand-in-hand. It is for this reason they experiment with many kinds of new technology. Many of the technologies prove beneficial and hence are used extensively. Often technology is perceived as the vehicle which might boost the company into a commanding position *vis-à-vis* their competitors.

(3) *The learner.* This is the kind of organization who sees technology as a potential boon but is somewhat cautious about how and when it could be introduced. They would like to learn from the mistakes of the innovators but, concomitantly, do not want to wait too long to introduce the technology. Their often heard motto is 'we do not want to be left behind'. They also feel it is important to 'get on the learning curve'. Technology is something which can be acquired, but to learn how to use it to its fullest requires a great deal of time and experience. Further, as technology advances it becomes harder and harder for the uninitiated to obtain its full value (or some may argue, any value at all). Therefore, it is important to acquire technology for its experimental value.

# A Composite Theory of Electronic Office Information Growth in Organizations

Based on our models of the five stages of growth in electronic office information systems and organizational approaches to information technology, we propose a more complete theory of growth. The basic stages in the growth curve are the five stages described above. The difference, however, is in the *shape* of the growth curve and is dependent upon the particular organizational information technology approach adopted by the organization. Figures 1, 2 and 3 project the growth of electronic office information systems based on the three categories of organizational information technology approach.

## Discussion

In case one, the procrastinator, the level of growth of electronic office information systems is very much less and slower than in the other two cases. Organizations adopting this approach will find they are spending a relatively long period of time in stage one—initiation—and stage three—control, and much shorter periods in stages two and four—contagion and integration. This is based on their inherent nature of conservatism and extreme caution in the face of change.

Case two is very different—somewhat the opposite of case one—in terms of growth of office technology. Of the three, organizations adopting this approach will experience the steepest and greatest growth of electronic office information systems. They will spend relatively short periods of time in stages one and three—the cautious stages—and long periods in stages two and four—the growth stages. They will also reach maturity more quickly than their counterparts.

Case three, the learner, experiences the smoothest growth of the three, spending roughly the same period of time in each stage. The level of growth of

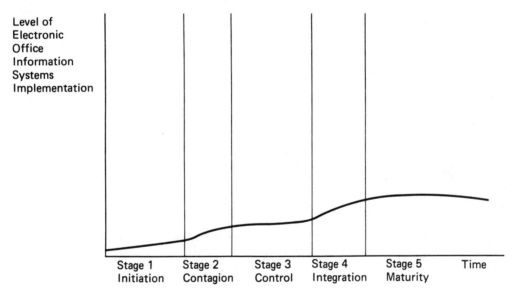

Figure 1. Case 1—the procrastinator

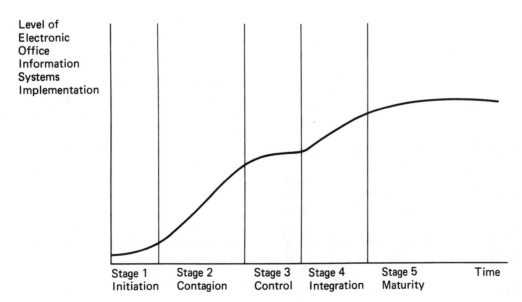

Figure 2. Case 2—the innovator

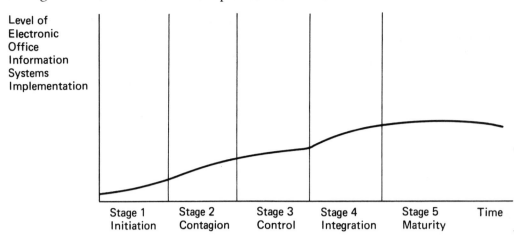

Figure 3. Case 3—the learner

electronic office information systems will not be as great nor as fast as the innovator but more than that of the procrastinator. The learner will also tend to reach maturity quicker than the procrastinator but slower than the innovator.

Three additional points must be made. First, these cases are really archetypes. No organization will exhibit all the characteristics of any particular case exactly as described; there will inevitably be some variations. In some organizations, various departments will no doubt move through the stages more quickly than others. For example, a number of the more adventuresome departments may advance rapidly through stages one and two before they contend with an organization-wide scrutiny of office technological growth in stage three. Other departments, during the same period of time, may have remained in stage one. This poses no serious problem for the organization; it has acquired the valuable technological learning from those advanced technological departments which can then be disseminated to other departments. Further, the acquired technological learning will be used to develop policies and strategies for the stages of control and integration. In fact, it is not until the third and fourth stages are reached, that an organization really has enough knowledge (acquired from technological learning) to base an electronic office information systems strategy on. Prior to these stages, any office systems strategies must be limited in scope and/or general in nature because the required knowledge will not be available. Thus, organizational long range planning for electronic office information systems must initially be more limited and general in nature. Then, after a number of departments have gone through the first two stages, a more strategic and integrative plan can be developed.

Second, an organization can show signs of moving from one case to another at various points in time. It does not *always* have to be either an innovator, procrastinator or learner. For some technologies it may take one approach, but for other technologies, a different approach. Similarly, an organization

may start off as, say, a learner but switch to an innovator or procrastinator during the second or third stage. Our electronic office information systems growth theory does concede the possibility of some movement between approaches. Nevertheless, we feel the archetypes described in this paper are broad enough to permit the various movements (of which some will inevitably take place) to occur without destroying the validity of the general organizational scenarios these archetypes depict.

Third, we attach a neutral organizational value of all the approaches. That is, none of these approaches are advocated as *the* best one. The approach an organization should adopt in addressing the growth of electronic office information systems is very much dependent on a number of issues; for example: the age and size of the organization, its past history, the organizational climate, managerial 'style', etc. (see also the eleven considerations cited earlier in the paper). Some organizations find themselves in relatively stable environments and have therefore adopted a company policy of conservatism. To recommend a policy for office technology growth based on an innovator framework, might cause the organization innumerable problems. The approach adopted must reflect the organization's overall policy and method of operation.

## Conclusions

This paper has had two central purposes. First, to suggest that as organizations move inexorably into the information age, electronic office information systems will play an increasingly important role in helping organizations adapt to the change. Electronic office information systems are ideally suited to meet the changing needs of the organizations as they attempt to cope with the trends involved in the coming information age.

Second, organizations need to know how to plan or build a strategy for electronic office information systems. A composite stage theory has been proposed which is based on Nolan's stage theory of data processing growth. The result is three cases or scenarios reflecting different electronic office information systems growth curves. With this information, organizations should be better able to develop a strategy for dealing with new information technology.

The future of the office systems area promises to be an interesting one as vendors jockey for position, new technology is developed, new applications are thought of, and the social and organizational problems are tackled. Make no mistake about it, electronic office information systems are not just a passing fad. They are for real as are their consequences. Organizations who approach electronic office information systems with this knowledge and an awareness of a need for a strategy for them will be in a better position to take advantage of the technology.

## References

(1) J. Galbraith, *Designing Complex Organizations*, Addison-Wesley (1973).

(2) K. Nygaard, The impact of social movements, *The Computer Journal*, **23** (1), 19–22 (1980).

(3) M. Zisman, Office automation: revolution or evolution, *Sloan Management Review*, Spring (1978).

(4) S. Price, *Introducing the Electronic Office*, NCC Publications, Manchester (1979).

(5) S. Coates, *The Office of the Future*, Department of Communications, Goverment of Canada, Ottawa (1981).

(6) M. Hammer and M. Sirbu, What is office automation?, *Proceedings of the 1980 Office Automation Conference*, Atlanta, Georgia, 3–5 March, pp. 37–49 (1980).

(7) C. Ellis, Information control nets. A mathematical model of office information flow, *Proceedings of the 1979 Conference on Simulation, Measurement and Modelling of Computer Systems*, pp. 225–239 (1979).

(8) H. Mintzberg, *The Nature of Managerial Work*, Harper & Row Publishers, New York (1973).

(9) C. Gibson and R. Nolan, Managing the four stages of EDP growth, *Harvard Business Review*, pp. 76–88, January–February (1974).

(10) R. Nolan, Managing the crises in data processing, *Harvard Business Review*, pp. 115–126, March–April (1979).

(11) R. Hirschheim, Information management planning in organizations, LSE Working Paper, 81-08-01 (1981).

(12) R. Hirschheim, *Office Automation: Concepts, Technologies and Issues*, Addison-Wesley (forthcoming).

# Information Technology—Its Impact on Property Development

*B. C. Burrows, Senior Consultant, Futures Information Associates, Milton Keynes*

*The history of the factory system is briefly dealt with and the impact of the systems building approach and the Advance Factory Unit is discussed. The needs of the new technology are examined in relation to research for factories, science parks and offices. The lack of information and its fragmentation is noted. One of the largest barriers to new development in Information Technology is the lack of a new Use Class for industry and offices combined. The implementation of the ORBIT report on the property market is discussed and recommendations for future action are proposed.*

## Introduction

There is a consensus view, that with the impact of information technology and flexible manufacturing systems job loss in industry will be considerable. Forecasts have been made of a similar nature for the office sector. Other forecasts state that job loss will be less here than for the manufacturing sector. This is because there will be an increase in services many of which are labour intensive. As these will be, in many cases, office based it is likely therefore that job loss here will not be as great as for other sectors.

However, unemployment rates will remain high and this will challenge the whole basis of our culture both for the capitalist and communist sectors. Both cultures are based on the concept of the importance of work. This is expressed in Max Weber's concept of the Protestant work ethnic and Marx's theory of surplus value. Unemployment is concealed in the Soviet Union in a number of ways. One can take a pessimistic view of this, in fact, that it will undermine our cultural base. This, however, has happened before when the scientific revolution undermined the values of medieval society. Another view is that the problems facing us will make the division between East and West meaningless. For Das Capital we will have Das Information. If this view is correct then any impediments on the take up of the new technology should be studied and plans made to alter the situation. Many of these problems are long term and as yet no firm guidelines can be established. However, one of the current barriers to the development of the new technology is the lack of suitable premises.

## The Immediate Problem

Although we know that the impact of information technology will destroy more jobs than it will create it is essential that this take up is done with the greatest possible speed. The country or region such as Europe which establishes the largest market share of this sector will have:

(1) Higher employment than other areas.

(2) The wealth which can be used to solve problems caused by a changing society.

However, there are a number of factors slowing up the use of the new technology. These are:

(1) lack of suitable premises;

(2) lack of people with the necessary skills;

(3) social attitudes which resist change.

When one attempts to find out why we do not have, as yet, enough premises suitable for high technology, it is found that items (2) and (3) play an important role in this.

## Lack of Suitable Premises for Information Technology

### Factories—History

The source of the word is uncertain but it developed from the word factor and was in use before the industrial revolution. These were small buildings often in villages based in water power. The industrial revolution was caused by steam power

---

The author is Senior Consultant, Futures Information Associates, 39 Vicarage Street, Woburn Sands, Milton Keynes MK17 8RE.

with the resulting location of large factory units in urban areas. There is a great deal of contemporary literature on the design of machinery but none that I have traced on design of factory buildings. These were often several stories high and appear to be based on local vernacular design. Isolated examples can be found of good design for industrial buildings but in general not much thought was given to this.

## More Recent Developments

Electric light and electric power transmission become major influences in factory design. Also the development of mild steel as a structural material resulted in changing factory buildings. However, the concepts which demanded thinking were:

(1) layout of machinery;

(2) working conditions.

Little thought was given to factory design as a total concept.[1]

## The Current Industrial Scene

About 50 per cent of British factory stock was built before World War II and approximately 25 per cent of this stock since 1967. Most of these buildings were expensive to heat due to lack of insulation.[2] Little attempt has been made to study factory design and establish concepts for improvements. This should be seen in relation to the planning laws. The concept of systems building for industry and the Advance Factory Unit will be dealt with later.

## Planning Legislation

Before 1947 there was little control of building development. We have seen that the industrial revolution established industrial buildings in urban areas with little thought of the impact on living conditions in these areas. The concept of planning developed from concern over health hazards due to lack of sanitation. The result was the establishment of sewage and sanitation systems.

In 1947 the first Town and Country Planning Act[3] was published. This defined the use to which land could be used and thus controlled the growth and location of industry and commerce. This act was revised in 1971 and published as Town and Country Planning England and Wales. The relevant sectors for industry and commerce is the Use Classes Order.

These are as follows:

Class II    Use as an office for any purpose.

Class II    Use as a light industrial building for any purpose.

Class IV    Use as a general industrial building for any purpose.

Class V    Special industrial group A: use in connection with alkalis.

Class VI    Special industrial group B: six headings ranging from smelting to chromium plating.

Class VII    Special industrial group C: seven headings ranging from burning of bricks to production of inorganic pigments.

Class VIII    Special industrial group D: ten headings covering distilling and blending of oil, rubber and acids.

Class IX    Special industrial group E: numerous noxious trades of which the most quoted is bone boiler!

Class X    Use as a wholesale warehouse or repository for any purpose.

It will be seen that these use classes orders are a serious barrier to the development of premises suitable for the new technology with its greatest constraint on local authorities. The New Towns and the Regional Development Corporations have in many cases been able to get around this legislation.

## Factory Design

Little attempt has been made to study factory design and establish concepts for improvement. The first major overview was a series of articles by Jolyon Drury in the *Architects Journal* under the heading AJ. Handbook of Factory Design.[4] In this the author deals with all aspects of factory design and the wider issues such as planning controls, the environment, building types, fire precautions, safety etc.

The most interesting section is on building types.[5] These are seen as follows.

Industrial building purpose types:

1.01 From detailed examination of the demands made by each industry type, most can be accommodated in one of five categories:

1.    Light production and assembly;
      because of the wide difference of demands on buildings in this sector, it is divided into:
      (a) high technology;
      (b) low technology;

2.    batch production and assembly;

3.    mass production and assembly;

4.    process-based production;

This sector also requires subdividing into two purpose groups:
(a) centralized facility;
primary and secondary processing on one site (see the glossary for definitions—paras 2.04 and 2.05);
(b) dispersed facility;
primary and secondary processing on different sites;

5.     heavy engineering.

The section which is of most interest to us is 1(a) high technology. The author concludes that 'there is often a demand for interchangeability between office, laboratory, production and storage space' and 'this type can result in a building form more allied to office or laboratory practice'. Multi-storey developments are possible.[6]

## The Advance Factory Unit (AFU)

The idea of the AFU was conceived by the new town movement. This was to build a factory in advance of demand in order to attract industry and employment to the designated area. In this they were very successful. An estimate of the requirements of industry in 1972 came to the conclusions that the AFU supplied the needs of 75 per cent of industry. Edward D. Mills[7] the author of this work wrote

> It has been estimated that the multi-purpose open approach to industrial buildings could produce a type of structure that would meet the requirement of 75 per cent of the manufacturing industry of this country and only the remaining quarter would require special accommodation tailored to its peculiar requirement.

Since this was written the changes in industry have been considerable and this change is still continuing at an ever increasing pace.

## Systems Building for Industry and the AFU

Due to new structural methods the concept of systems building was developed both for industrial, commercial and domestic building. Although this is still used the claims made for this style of building were not fully realized as it was a completely technical approach with little thought for the needs of the people using the buildings.[8] However, it did have a major influence on the building of AFU's within the New Towns.

Not a great deal has been published on this. Most AFU's used this method of construction but due probably to the rivalry between the New Towns details of design procedures were not widely available.

In 1972, Milton Keynes Development Corporation published *Systems Building for Industry*[9] which formed the basis for their AFU strategy. This was an attempt to identify what types of industry there were and to design buildings to meet their needs. It is a well researched document but it shows the weakness in research when only the past is researched and conclusions drawn. For example the needs of the electrical industry are described and attempts made to meet their needs. There is no mention of the electronics industry which at the time was growing fast in the United Kingdom. In fact at the time we were supplying the needs of this country without a large import of electronic components: the large import penetration of electronic based goods was due to our neglect of innovation, design and marketing.

## The AFU and High Technology

When I first saw an AFU in 1975 I realized that they would not be suitable for high technology. These were general purpose buildings suitable for all needs. We have seen that in this they were successful but to continue building them in large quantities would be disastrous because the needs of high technology were not met. They also lacked insulation so that the high rise in energy costs resulted in great energy loss. Work at the Open University energy research team have estimated that 50 per cent of energy used in industry is in heating the building.

The reason why these buildings did not meet the needs of the new technology based industries are as follows:

(1) high eaves—in most cases about 18 ft.;

(2) lack of office space—at most 10 per cent sometimes none at all;

(3) poor insulation;

(4) in some cases poor locations.

Therefore it is likely that the stock of AFU's in the United Kingdom is at a level to meet demand. These will be used for light engineering and mainly warehousing.

The question which needs to be asked is can they be converted for the high tech industries. The answer is yes by installing a mezzanine floor and improved insulation. However, care in conversion is needed here because location is important. IT companies local in areas near to motorway junctions and to airports. Also the surrounding environment is vital. As well as this these firms cluster together. Most high technology firms would not locate in an area devoted to warehousing.

## The Reaction of the New Town Movement

The response of the New Town Movement to the recession was to undertake target marketing. In this, research was done to identify growth areas in the economy, identify organizations within these sectors and then approach them. Previous to this mail shots were undertaken which was both wasteful and ineffective. The concept is in fact what the Japanese have done on a national and international scale. In fact there is a lesson here both for industry, government and local authorities to promote similar schemes in the United Kingdom.

At Milton Keynes as a result of research the following areas were identified in the following order.

Electronic Components
Computers and Software
Office Equipment (including word processors)
Information Technology as a whole

The emphasis is now on communications and networking in relation to computers, work stations, data bases and cable.

During discussions with the electronic component manufacturers in 1979 it was found that in most cases these firms liked Milton Keynes but did not like the AFU's. Therefore attempts were made to obtain funding for more suitable premises. In most cases these buildings as well as office development are funded by pension funds and insurance companies. However, it was found that most of the funding organizations only wished to fund a general purpose building which they thought would be suitable for all needs. They did not realize that times were changing. The first organization to fund suitable premises in Milton Keynes was Sun Alliance. They have funded a number of pavilion style buildings in Milton Keynes at Linford Wood Business Centre.[10] They have also funded a development at Swindon. This has made the breakthrough and some other funding bodies have followed this.

## The Response from Industry

Industry does not seem to be well organized to make its views known although the CBI has improved its image in recent years. The views of industry are often expressed on an informal basis or via NEDO and do not get documented in many cases, or else are not widely circulated. However, in a report in 1981 from the National Electronics Council the following conclusions were given.[11]

One of the major problems in this country for high technology manufacturing companies is the availability of suitable accommodation. The vast majority of industrial buildings being erected in this country by both the private and public sectors, are warehouse type with over 5 m headroom and only 10 per cent of it office accommodation. For most high technology companies up to 50 per cent of the accommodation has to be reasonable appointed office or assembly areas. The nearest type of the accommodation has to be reasonably but it is normally forbidden to manufacture in this sort of building.

So far I have not seen any evidence from the CBI. They should set up a committee and issue a report on this.

## The Reaction of the Chartered Surveyors

The commercial surveyors were made aware of this problem because they could not find suitable premises for high technology enterprises and thus lost business. Therefore firms had a choice.

(1) Build a special purpose unit.

(2) Not expand or relocate.

Attempts were made to influence the funding organizations by making reference to these problems in journals such as *The Estates Times* and *Estates Gazette*. However, this had little influence and was followed by a series of reports based on research done by or commissioned by the commercial estate agents.

The first report was by Herring Son and Daw.[12] It was based on a survey undertaken by *Computer Weekly* and some research done by Conran Roche, planning and design consultants in Milton Keynes. Most are ex-members of staff of the Development Corporation including Fred Lloyd Roche who was General Manager of MKDC.

The result of an analysis of supply and demand was that:

(1) For the large national or international groups wishing to establish integrated facilities including R & D it was found that there was little suitable accommodation.

(2) For the small local company who in most cases needs small units there was little available accommodation.

The case of Prime Computers, a large international company who manufacture in the U.S.A., was cited. Their requirements are given as follows.

Being an American company and willing to spend the money on the right sort of building we were looking for:

Campus style building 1/2 storeys.

Ample car parking (in this business everyone has a car!).

An internal environment conducive to high technology highly-paid creative people.

A good environment (outlook) and image.

Good communications (motorways).

Eventually we did find an architect and a location (Milton Keynes) that fitted the bill. We only had one Pension Fund that even showed a casual interest. Their first question was 'Can it be divided up for sub-letting?' followed by 'We'd prefer it to be on an industrial estate'. Their final contribution to creating good places to work was 'The design is a bit unconventional—we'd prefer it to be standard width'. (The design was almost identical to 10–15 year old designs common in the Boston area of the U.S.)

The results of a series of questions for firms looking for premises were as follows:

|  | % |
| --- | --- |
| Lack of suitable premises | 64 |
| Local planning restrictions | 24 |
| Difficulty obtaining planning consent | 11 |
| Cost | 23 |
| Landlord's refusal of mixed use | 7 |
| Length of lease | 14 |

An analysis of existing buildings by age revealed that about 20 per cent are now over 25 years old. Only 12 per cent of buildings have been constructed to occupiers own specifications, the remainder being general purpose buildings. However, for firms with over 100 employees it was found that 30 per cent had buildings designed to their requirements. This is illustrated in Figure 1.

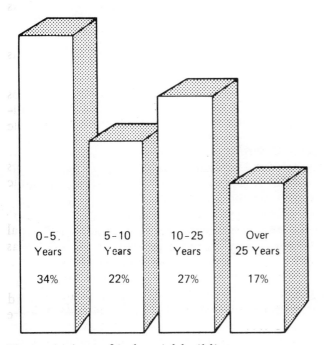

Figure 1. Age of industrial buildings

Next the question was asked why companies may wish to move and their reasons are as follows:

Reasons for a move

| Reason | Numerical (%) | Weighted (%) |
| --- | --- | --- |
| Lack of space | 94 | 81 |
| Rental costs | 70 | 40 |
| Rates | 48 | 23 |
| Staff availability | 61 | 42 |
| Transport facilities | 34 | 19 |
| Poor design | 34 | 17 |
| Cost of conversion | 27 | 14 |
| Environment | 22 | 11 |
| Landlords' refusal for change of use | 10 | 6 |

In a more recent survey Herring and Daw[13] asked the following question about the finding of suitable premises and the answers were as follows:

|  | (%) |
| --- | --- |
| Without difficulty | 21 |
| Not at all | 16 |
| After some difficulty | 29 |
| After major alterations | 34 |

It will be seen that the situation is improving but not fast enough if we are to create the necessary wealth needed to solve our considerable social problems.

This report came to the conclusion that the Use Class Order should be amended to include a new class to read 'Use for a combination of office, research and development, light industrial and wholesale warehouses uses where no one of these uses is more than 50 per cent of the whole'. In my view the reference to light industrial and warehousing is not necessary as there is enough property available for the needs of these sectors.

Since then there has been one more important report on the needs of modern technology by Debenham Tewson and Chinnocks.[14] In the report the conclusion is reached that High Tech is a meaningless phrase. It is used both as a style of architecture and as a type of business. Both are not capable of precise definition.

Therefore this report suggests knowledge based industries. This would therefore include biotechnology as well as electronics and IT. It also would include any new industries which will arise.

Many modern industries are not very interested in the design of property. Small firms are willing to camp out in order to save costs. They are also only interested in leasing for short periods. As they mature and grow they become more property conscious with more interest in ownership.

Their main interest is in the location of the business.

## Influences on Location (U.K.)

| Criteria | | Mentioned by (%) |
|---|---|---|
| Access to | motorway network | 52 |
| | Specialist/skilled staff | 49 |
| | Support staff | — |
| | Suppliers | — |
| | Markets | 30 |
| | Good residential environment | 28 |
| | International airport | 25 |
| | Domestic airport | 14 |
| | University/polytechnic | 12 |
| | Cultural/recreational facilities | 9 |
| | Railway network | 7 |
| | None of the above | 5 |

The low rating of 25 per cent for airports is surprising. It is suggested that this is an important factor in the thinking of the top executive but not so important in the day to day operation of the business. The low rating for links with universities is not surprising and could explain the low take up of innovation in the U.K.

Sixty-five per cent of firms were not willing to pay higher rent in this area for improved accommodation.

It will be seen from the table below the key factor is flexibility in design.

## Attractive Features of Individual Buildings

| Factor | Score (%) |
|---|---|
| Design flexibility | 26 |
| Planning flexibility | 21 |
| Attractive financial package | 16 |
| Potential for expansion | 15 |
| Right sized units | 15 |
| Image/prestige | 12 |
| Short leases | 9 |
| Good natural lighting | 5 |

This means that what is required is a shell which can be used for any activity with the ability to change.

It is concluded that knowledge based industries are less concerned with building design than traditional industries. This contradicts the findings of other research reports. One explanation is that for start up knowledge based industries costs are vital. Many of these start in houses, garages and garden sheds. It raises the importance of low cost small units being available. As the company becomes successful and grows they could become more interested in good design in order to project an image. This could explain the contradictory findings of this report in relation to others.

However, the view was expressed that eaves over 18 ft were unsuitable for modern industry.

There is a large amount of high tech property not let, the reason being is that it is in the wrong area in depressed areas. Property investors are still not interested in investing in property for the knowledge based industries. The percentage of investment in property is

Pension funds 11 per cent
Insurance companies 15 per cent.

Attitudes are changing slowly but it is thought that this will not be enough to meet the needs of the knowledge based industries.

The concept of factory and office will disappear in that one flexible multi purpose building will be needed. The Planning Use Classes Order is out of date and a new use class is needed.

In conclusion the most important factors are seen as:

Good communications, i.e. motorways
Good environment
Supply of locally based skilled labour.

I would add the building of factories either with eaves less than 18 ft or with an upper storey for office use as a factor as important as the above conclusions.

## Small Units

The above report mentions the importance of the availability of small units. These are vital for start up industries many of which have a high technology base.

Small business consists mainly of the following:

Firms making 'widgets' at lower overheads than large firms
Firms making 'widgets' under sub contracts
Firms engaged in the service sector
Firms in the area of new technology

In most cases the last sector is how new technology starts and grows. As an example the founders of Apple Computers started work in a garage. There is a great shortage of small units which is an inhibiting factor in establishing new businesses. The reason for this is because of costs. If one let a 30,000 sq ft factory to one client administrative costs are low. However, if this unit was divided into lots of 500 sq ft administrative costs would rise steeply. In the 1980 Budget changes were made so that in a 100 per cent building allowance could be obtained for development. This has made the situation much better and these units are coming onto the market. There is a small business unit at Kiln Farm in Milton Keynes and other areas have similar schemes.

In 1982 the Department of Industry published a document[15] which studied this problem and an attempt was made to see if this allowance had improved the situation. The position from 1978 to 1981 is as shown in Figure 2.

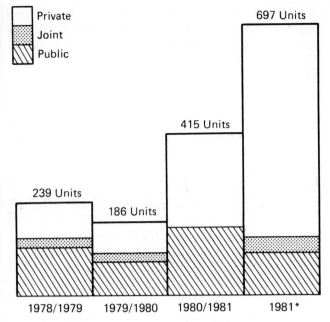

Figure 2. Starts of small industrial units by financial years

It will be seen that this has had a major effect on the supply of small units. It is essential that if we are to have a high take up of innovative firms the supply of small units should be closely monitored and any demand promptly met.

## Redundant Industrial Property

King and Co.[16] monitor the demand for industrial property on a continuous basis. Therefore it is possible to know how much vacant industrial property there is in a national and regional basis. Property under 5000 sq ft is excluded so it is not possible to monitor the demand for smaller units but we have already seen that this is considerable: buildings under construction are also monitored.

The conclusions are that there is a large number of older property which will not be let. Much of this was built many years ago but it could apply to the older AFU's. These are not letting as well as the newer high tech units.

One answer would be to convert them into a two storey building by the use of a mezzanine floor. They could therefore be of interest to the high tech user in most cases who needs 50 per cent office space. We have seen that high tech firms will only locate in an area if the following factors are present.

(1) Good environment.

(2) Access to motorway and airport.

(3) Local skilled labour.

(4) Other firms of a similar nature in the immediate area.

If some of these factors are present then conversion could be worth while. If not the answer is to divide up their units into smaller areas suitable for small firms. This could interest the start up innovative firm as we have seen that they only become concerned about their image and environment when they could afford to do so.

If no action is taken most of the vacant property will be used for warehousing and not manufacture. Warehousing is important but does not employ many people. Also with a low manufacturing base warehousing increases with stocks of imported goods.

## AFU Building Programme

It is essential that this is scaled down because of lower demand. This problem has been realized by the New Town movement. In fact in Milton Keynes most new industrial development is ground lease or freehold for high technology firms. English Industrial Estates and the development agencies in Scotland and Wales are also aware of the problem. The danger is that many local authorities are not, and are continuing to build AFU's which will either stay empty or be used for warehousing. The supply of warehousing needs to be carefully monitored because oversupply can help import penetration by making it easier to stock goods from abroad and help their distribution.

An interesting example is a statement to the local paper by Thamesdown chief executive David Kent. Thamesdown covers the Swindon area. He is quoted as saving.[17]

The main reason for the continuing upward trend in empty properties is an increase in the number of older and out-of-date buildings in the borough, according to Thamesdown's chief executive, David Kent. He said there were now a number of older industrial premises which were unsuitable for new high technology firms moving to the town.

Swindon is a natural innovation area due to the M4 corridor but if local authorities in other areas wish to attract new industries they will have to examine their industrial building programme with a great deal of care.

## The Rise of the Science Park

The science park was an attempt to:

(1) link academic research with innovation and production by proximity;

(2) establish manufacturing conditions to office standards.

Silicon Valley grew out of a science park set up by Stanford University as the Stanford Industrial Park.[18]

The first to be established in the United Kingdom was at Cambridge which has been very successful. Cambridge can now be considered to be an innovative area. Other Universities have plans to undertake similar enterprises and these could be most useful in getting new products to the market place in the United Kingdom and for export.

However, it is a great pity that the term is being misused. For example there are 82 science parks in over 28 states in the U.S.A., of which only 19 are parks limited to science based industries. In the Drivers Jonas report[19] those in the United Kingdom are studied in some detail and the conclusion is drawn that the impact in new design should improve future trends and raise standards.

In the United Kingdom some local authorities have used the term for what is in fact a standard AFU. This is a great pity because there has been a reaction to use of this term with alternative names suggested such as industrial park, office park, innovation zone. Therefore if further science parks are to be planned it is important to make it clear that it is the linking of academic research to the market place. This is also of benefit to the academic as it is a two way learning process.

## The Impact of IT on the Central Business District

With the use of science parks many organizations will undertake research, manufacturing and head office administration in a pleasant rural location. Their presence in the Central Business District will be in the form of a regional sales office. Therefore the Central Business District will be dominated by the service sector with a strong bias towards financial services. Therefore the design of office buildings in this area should reflect these needs.

There is also the propect of a changing work pattern. The Americans call this telecommuting due to the fact that with the use of microcomputers being used as a terminal for on line searching it is now possible to work from home. The question is how many will wish to do so as it could alter the domestic design requirements for future house building. What is likely is that people will spend some time at home during the week and the rest in the office of factory. It is interesting that a large proportion of the Business Environmental Study group, a group with the Society for Strategic and Long Range Planning, work from home.

A recent report published by Beta Exhibition[20] as a result of a survey found that there is an expectation for more people to be working from home in the future. In 5 years time this could be as high as 40 per cent. It was based on a survey carried out by Korn/Ferry International for Beta Exhibitions of 255 companies listed in the *Times 1000 Directory* and *Jordan's Directory of Britain's Top 500 Electronic and Electrical Companies*. If these predictions come true there is a major challenge for the urban planner in relation to urban renewal.

## The Evolution of the Office

There have been many attempts to define the concept of an office but basically it is a means of receiving, recording, processing and the transmission of information. Therefore it will be seen that the electronic or automated office will radically change the operation methods, not the function of the office. The concept of the paperless office is most likely a myth or a long way away but the impact of IT will both change the way an office operates and the type and design of building required. In fact an office need not be a building. It can be a car or hotel room in the case of the travelling salesman. The first offices were linked to the merchant and were in their homes. Later these transactions were to move to the coffee houses. Some of the first office buildings were built for government and were occupied by civil servants.

The factory became the focal point for urban development with houses being built around for convenience. Later both industrial and domestic development was to move out to peripherals of the town and offices moved in. The Central Business District had arrived. Much more attention was given to the design of offices as they became a commercial prestige symbol. The skyscraper offices of New York are an example. Many of the top architects were involved in these developments. For example as early as 1904 Frank Lloyd Wright designed the Larking Building in Buffalo, New York.

## The Evolution of the Office

*The Impact of IT on Office Design*
In 1982 Richard Ellis[21] published the results of a survey on this subject. This survey was based on questions sent out to 500 office users in London with a further 100 in Manchester.

Their conclusions are as follows:

(1) From our survey of occupiers of modern offices in central city locations, we found no evidence that office space had been reduced as a result of the use of new microchip based equipment—when there had been opportunity to do so.

(2) There is no evidence that floorspace requirements will be reduced over the next 5 years because of usage of the new equipment.

(3) Occupiers who have moved to larger premises were found to have a higher than average usage of word processors.

(4) No link can therefore be established at the present time between the application of microchip equipment to office work and a reduction in demand for accommodation.

(5) The demand for office space is more closely associated with business expansion or contraction than any other factor.

(6) The majority of occupiers are not yet using microchip equipment but an increasing intention to do so in the future is apparent.

(7) There are good grounds for anticipating that any floor space released by the introduction of microchip equipment will not become surplus to requirements but will be re-utilized by redesigning the office layout.

(8) The microchip's effect on demand must be kept in perspective. The trend of growth in the service sector of the economy has had more effect on demand than the microchip and it is the future outlook for this sector to which research on office demand should be particularly directed.

These conclusions are of considerable interest but the fact that it was based on a very small sample should be borne in mind.

However, an interesting layout of the impact of IT on office layout is included (Figure 3).

There is also some discussion on the impact of IT on office design and employment.

This illustrates an office of 6500 sq ft.

(1) Pre IT there are 60 occupants at 108 sq ft per person.

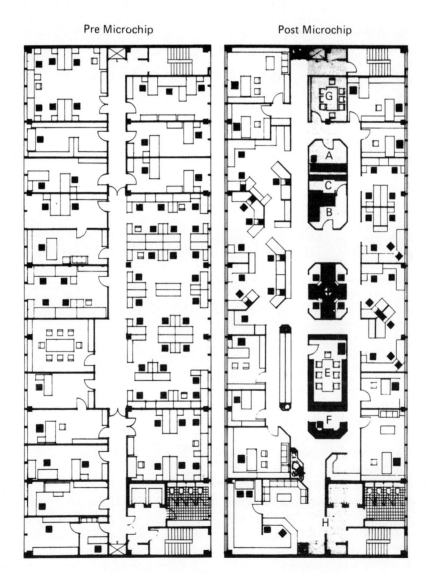

Pre Microchip     Post Microchip

A Printer and Telex Room
B Central Processor Room
C Secure Data and Programming Store
D Main Data Input Terminals and Electronic Filing Units
E Audio Visual meeting Studio with Facsimile Terminal
F Main Paper Copiers, Collators and Microfilm Records
G Internal Meeting Room
H Central Bulkhead Duct (Shaded Area)

Figure 3

(2) Post IT there are 45 occupants at 144 sq ft per person.

This is a decline in employment of about 20 per cent.

An issue of the *AJ*[22] was devoted to the relationship between IT and the architect. An article about this on workspace made the following points:

(1) there will be an increase in the amount of space per person;

(2) less space for individual work stations but more space for meeting areas;

(3) less workspace per person as staff had to spend more time working from home or out of the office;

(4) these will be smaller and more fluid working groups;

(5) space for IT equipment will take up to 30 per cent of the total area.

A more recent and most detailed study published is the CALUS Report.[23] This report opens with an attempt to quantify the office market. Figures are quoted showing that office employment showed a steady increase from 1961 to 1981 and that despite attempts of Governments to decentralize the stock of offices mainly remain in the south east with 55 per cent of England's office space, 38 per cent of which is in London.

The concept of IT is then discussed and the reasons for making the decision of office automation is seen as:

Improved services, 93 per cent.
New services, 62 per cent.
Increased productivity, 76 per cent.
Reduced office space, 19 per cent.
Improved job satisfaction, 7 per cent.

It is stated that in the last 18 months there has been a 30 per cent decline in office lettings. It is highly likely that this is due to the recession and not IT.

So far IT has not resulted in a large number of redundancies. In fact where there has been office automation the staff who have been replaced by its use have found alternative work because new jobs have been recreated due to an increase in the level of business.

It is thought that there will not be a rapid decline in demand for office space as job loss will be compensated by the allocation of more floorspace per office worker.

The change in office design will be considerable. False ceilings and raised floors will be needed to accommodate the increasing use of wiring. Also more flexible lighting will be needed to reduce glare

from VDU's. The fact that IT equipment gives off heat should also be noted.

Design in general will have to be more flexible and the concept of the shell building is mentioned. This is being used more in the U.S.A. and should be used here, but opposition is foreseen to this in the U.K. In the study on office location IT is seen as not having an important direct effect but it will extend the range of alternative sites. Within the next 5–10 years there will be an increase in locating in more decentralized areas which are more environmentally attractive.

The investment market will be affected in the following manner:

(1) It will increase uncertainty in the office market.

(2) Investors will look for more security.

(3) Investors will accept shorter lease and be ready to accept multiple occupancy.

(4) Locations in an enhanced environment will be of increasing importance.

(5) Flexibility of design will become of increasing importance with the basic shell concept being adopted.

(6) In order to minimize risk in investment in new designs there will be a growth of syndicated funds.

It will be seen that this report is more concerned with levels of employment than office design although these two factors can not be studied in isolation.

There is one major study which is only concerned with the impact of IT and office design. This is the ORBIT Report.[24]

This is a multi-client research project sponsored by 10 organizations with an interest in IT, office equipment and office design and marketing. The research team included Duffy, Eley, Building Use Studies and Eosys Ltd.

The object of this study was to see if developments in office design were responding to the increased use of IT in an office environment, the timescale of the project being for the next 10 years to 1992.

It is concluded that this 10 year period will be one of the most critical for office development due to the following factors.

(1) Although most of the technology which will be used in the office in the next 10 years is available, how this will be used for future office work is not fully known.

(2) It is essential that office designs respond to the use of IT or buildings could be obsolete and unlettable.

It is essential therefore to establish guide lines for what type of office is needed in the future.

One aspect is that most pension funds have an increasing share of the property market. Therefore not only could unusuable offices effect economic activity, it could also affect levels of pensions.

The research project was divided into seven stages.

(1) Desk research in IT.

(2) Organizational case studies based in visits to 17 buildings.

(3) Building assessments.

(4) Information technology and organizational structure.

(5) Information technology and employment.

(6) Information technology and the office worker.

(7) Conclusions.

It is predicted that multi task work stations will be at the ratio of 1 for 6 workers within the next 5–10 years.

The paperless office will not happen as the use of paper may even increase.

Electronic filing will account for less than 50 per cent of stored documents for the next 15 years.

Contrary to popular belief, most unions had signed agreements on the use of IT. Their main concern was:

(1) to avoid redundancies;

(2) health and safety at work in relation to changes in the use of IT.

Most people using word processors found that this gave them greater job satisfaction.

The need for more flexible lighting, better designed furniture and the separation of VDU's from the keyboard is seen as essential and equipment manufacturers have been slow to respond. In fact there are many IT firms designing and marketing furniture for work stations.

Open plan is not popular and there has been a move away from this. The right to external views is now enshrined in the building regulations of several European centres.

## Employment Levels

The report does not deal in detail with employment levels in the office but it is concluded that the rapid growth in office staff will be halted. Jobs will be destroyed by IT i.e. clerks, but new jobs will be created by it, more middle level management. As yet there is no evidence as to which way this will go. There will either be a slow decline in employment or a very slight expansion. Work patterns will change. It is now possible to work from home. Contracting out work is done by Rank Xerox. It is thought that this will increase more than working from home i.e. self employed.

## Organizational Change

Centralized control over information will increase.

## Office Design

There is a lack of ducting for cable which is essential for use of IT. False floor or ceilings are a solution but British Telecom are not keen on false ceilings.

Better air conditioning systems are needed to reduce heat from IT equipment.

## Static and Dust

Static from carpets is a problem as well as dust from printers. Increased dust increases static. A solution is to use negative ion generators.

It is concluded that a main frame air conditioned room will still be needed.

Power surge possible from national grid is a problem. This can also be caused by use of in house equipment if use not phased.

The solution is dedicated circuits and line conditioning equipment, such as voltage transformers. Also stand by equipment is needed. Future—five sockets will be needed per worker.

## Demand for Office Space

The use of IT will be a new factor, more smaller offices needed.

More decentralization i.e. move from London. Due to use of IT as well as high rents and rates.

## How Building Must Respond

(1) Good air conditioning.

(2) Ability to be celluristic.

(3) Well considered perimeter for services and controls.

(4) Ability to accommodate large quantities of cabling i.e. trunking set in floors or raised floors.

This is a major research study and should be as widely known as possible and the implications taken note of by the property market. There are a large number of empty offices throughout the United Kingdom. If these are not built to the needs of the new technology they may never be let. It is clear that converting existing offices for the new technology is not easy.

## The Property Market as a Whole

We have seen that King and Co[16] attempt to measure the demand for industrial space. The only office space survey known to me is by Debenham Tewson and Chinnocks which only covers London by post codes.

The Department of the Environment[22] issued a survey of both commercial and industrial floor-space. This is divided into regions and is grouped under the headings for factories, warehouses, shops and restaurants and offices. Therefore it is possible to assess the total stock of non-domestic property in England. These figures are supplied to the DOE by the Inland Revenue who collect this information for rating assessments.

What we cannot tell from these figures is what type of property will be required for the future.

The Inland Revenue also undertake an assessment of the office market for Ministers in Government, this has just been made available to the public.[26] It should help in future research in the area as its findings can be considered to be unbiased.

However, it is still too early to assess how useful this will be in evaluating the market.

King and Co have just carried out a survey of the industrial market as a whole.[27] This includes some interesting findings as it shows that if the country as a whole is included the impact of IT is small. This with the impact of flexible manufacturing systems will increase greatly in the future.

One interesting finding is height of factory buildings. We have seen that IT firms require low eaves. Looking at the market as a whole the position is as follows:

Firms requiring eaves of 18 ft, 64 per cent.
Firms requiring eaves of 12 ft, 36 per cent.

There are two points to be considered here:

(1) The high proportion of warehousing.
(2) The need for low eaves buildings is much higher in innovative areas such as Bristol, Cambridge, Glenrothes and Milton Keynes.

The survey also includes some interesting figures (Figures 4 and 5).

These findings are mainly in line with previous reports.

In conclusion on the property market it must be said that research in this vital area is impeded due to:

(1) lack of information;
(2) what information sources there are fragmented with no focal point for reference.

The Royal Institution of Chartered Surveyors has the best information system but many of the publications do not come their way unless they are identified and request them. Much of this material does not get into the British Library. Also there is no on line data base on this subject. Therefore action is needed to establish a referral point for this, leading on to the setting up of an on line data base. Could the British Library and the Royal Institution of Chartered Surveyors set up a working part on this. This would consist of a working part from RICS and the research department of the British Library. Action is needed now in order to improve information resources in order to make people aware of this problem.

## The Attempts to Change the Class User Groups

We have seen that there is firm evidence to create a new class user group of an industrial/office complex. Since then there has been considerable pressure for a change with statements by Ministers indicating that a change is necessary.

In response to this, the Department of the Environment issued a circular Draft DOE Circular –/83.[28] In this they state that 'modern technological industries often require a mix of manufacturing, office, laboratory and other activities in their premises' and 'planning permission granted for such industrial development should not unduly restrict the occupiers' operational need to change the mix of activities in his premises'.

These are very fine sentiments of which no one will disagree but there is no recommendations for a new user class. This is completely essential if we are to maintain and increase our share of the large and growing world IT market. Fine words do not help when one has a battle with a bureaucracy which just follows the rules. This attitude is common both in the Civil Service and Local Government.

## Conclusions

The ORBIT Report, if their conclusions are followed through, means that much of the older offices and some of these being built now will never be let. If this is true the effect on the property

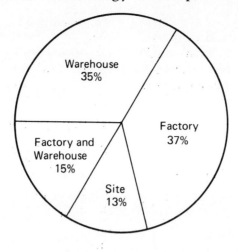

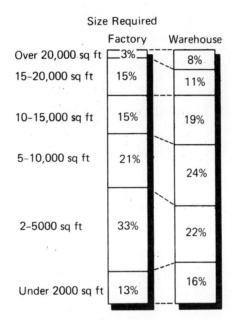

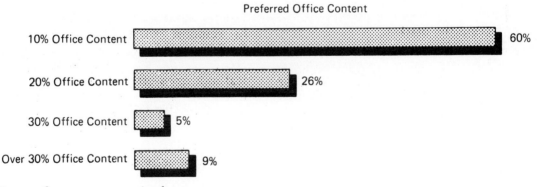

Figure 4. Type of property required

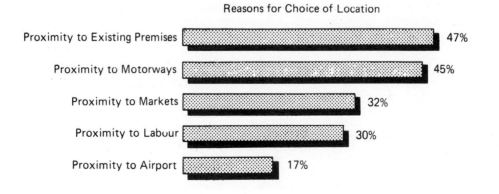

Figure 5.

market would be considerable. Much of the office market is funded by pension funds and insurance companies. This could adversely effect pensions and insurance policies. Also as many of these properties are in the older inner cities any urban renewal programme could be impared.

Therefore action is needed now in the following areas:

(1) set up a data base on the property market available for all researchers;

(2) establish a new user class;

(3) research to see if existing offices can be converted by the addition of raised floors or false ceiling or use of flat ribbon cable;

(4) implement the consensus view of the research for the needs of the IT industry as outlined in this article.

---

## References

(1) A.J. Handbook of Factory Design, *Architects Journal,* pp. 663–667, 5 October (1977).

(2) Ibid., p. 668.

(3) Town and country planning, England and Wales, *The Town and Country Planning 'Use classes',* Orders (1972).

(4) A.J. Handbook of Factory Design. A series of articles in the *Architects Journal* from 5 October (1977), later published in book form by Architectural Press.

(5) A.J. Handbook of Factory Design. *Architects Journal,* p. 869, 2 November (1972).

(6) Ibid., pp. 870–871.

(7) Edward D. Mills, The changing workplace, *Modern Technology and the Working Environment,* George Godwin Ltd. (1972).

(8) Andrew Rabneck, Whatever happened to the systems approach, *Architectural Design,* **46,** 67, 298–303, May (1976).

(9) Milton Keynes Development Corporation, *System Building for Industry* (1972); out of print.

(10) Linford Wood Business Centre. Pamphlet available from Milton Keynes Development Corporation or Sun Alliance.

(11) National Electronics Council, *Adapting to the Information Society* (1981).

(12) Herring Son and Daw, Property and technology, *The Needs of Modern Industry* (1982).

(13) Property for the electronics industry, *Estates Gazette,* pp. 918–919, 10 September (1983).

(14) Debenham Tewson and Chinnocks, *High Tech: Myths and Realities A Review of Developments for Knowledge-Based Industries* (1983).

(15) Department of Industry. Small Workshop Scheme. Survey of the effect of the 100 per cent Industrial Buildings Allowance, 10 pp. (1982).

(16) *King and Co. Industrial Floorspace Survey,* published three times a year.

(17) *Evening Advertiser,* p. 4, 21 December (1983); Swindon local paper.

(18) Annalee Saxerman, The Genesis of Silicon Valley, *Built Environment,* **1** (1), 7–17 (1982).

(19) James F. D. Williams, *A Review of Science Parks and High Technology Development,* Drivers Jonas (1982).

(20) Business Equipment Trends 1983/1984. Compiled by Kom/Ferry International for Beta Exhibitions Ltd., 8 Southampton Place, London WC1A 2EF.

(21) Richard Ellis Research Dependant. *The Impact of the Microchip on the Demand for Offices* (1982).

(22) The architect and information technology, *Architects Journal,* (whole issue) 25 August (1982).

(23) CALUS Research Report. *Property and Information Technology—The Future for the Office Market.* College of Estate Management, Reading (1983).

(24) ORBIT Report. *The Orbit Project, Findings, Conclusions and Recommendations.* Principle authors Francis Duffy, Dupley Eley Giffone Worthington with research by Eosys, p. 148 (1983).

(25) Department of the Environment, *Commercial and Industrial Floorspace Statistics, HMSO Regular Publications,* latest edition England (1978–1981).

(26) *The Inland Revenue Valuation Office Property Market Report,* published every 6 months by Surveyors Publications, 12 Great George Street, London SW1.

(27) *King and Co. Industrial Needs Survey, Property Business,* p. 74, December (1983).

(28) Department of the Environment Draft DOE Circular –/83 Industrial Development.

# Electronic Data Interchange: How Much Competitive Advantage?

*Robert I. Benjamin, David W. de Long and Michael S. Scott Morton*

The authors address the question of definitions in the evolving field or interorganizational systems and summarize some illustrative case studies. They examine the impact of EDI systems on suppliers and buyers and identify the critical factors that determine winners and losers in this area. They explore strategies for EDI pilot implementation and summarize the conclusions.

## (1) Introduction

The concept of gaining competitive advantage by linking organizations with information technology has taken on an overtone of dogma in many business circles in recent years. Early academic and media attention has focused on the sexy, high-impact interorganizational systems (IOS) that clearly have provided strategic advantage for their developers. Unfortunately, the reality of developing and maintaining electronic linkages between companies is not as easy or as profitable as the optimistic preaching of IOS advocates would lead us to believe.

There is no doubt that IOS can have a major impact on organizational performance and industry structure, but as the number of electronic linkages between companies increases those advantages are going to be harder to find and hold on to. Most of the literature to date in this field has relied on anecdotal data to draw conclusions about the conceptual development of interorganizational systems and their effects. To provide a more specific look at the issues and problems confronting organizations that implement a special class of IOS, known as electronic data interchange (EDI) systems, this paper draws on three detailed cases studies and other insights gained from MIT's Management in the 1990s Research Program.

Not surprisingly, our findings support some of the

previous conclusions about IOS in general, but they also raise new questions about the real impact of EDI systems on the organization and its competitive position. Implicit in the early writings on EDI has been the assumption that these systems hold great potential for providing strategic advantage. One of our conclusions, however, is that EDI applications, rather than being a competitive weapon, are increasingly a necessary way of doing business as illustrated by our three cases.

Thus, the majority of firms who undertake EDI projects as a competitive *necessity* must derive cost savings from these systems to cover the investment. But these savings can only come through the painful exercise of redesigning basic organizational structures and work processes. Unfortunately, it is hard to justify these very costly behavioural and organizational changes when only a small part of an organization's primary transaction volume is affected during the early stages of an EDI system. As we will see when we examine the three cases, there is logic in keeping EDI projects small at first and maintaining parallel systems. And gaining the high volume penetration of specific EDI applications needed to justify these systems has also proved difficult. Ultimately, the challenge will be to move EDI applications into high volume processing by creating new organizational structures and work processes that make the investment in this technology cost effective.

There is much to be learned from companies which have begun to use EDI technology. Nevertheless, even though other recent studies seem to support our findings (Emmelhainz, 1986), we realize there is always danger in generalizing about a new field like this, particularly from a relatively small sample. We recognize these risks, have tried to allow for them, and suggest only that the reader consider the relevance of our findings in the context of his or her own organization.

This paper is divided into seven sections. In

The authors are members of the Sloan School of Management at Massachusetts Institute of Technology.

Section 2, we will address the question of definitions in the evolving field of interorganizational systems. Until now, the definitions used have been general and relatively imprecise, but different classes of IOS, such as EDI, are beginning to emerge and they need to be differentiated. Section 3 summarizes the case studies used to illustrate our findings. Section 4 examines the impacts of EDI systems on both suppliers and buyers, and Section 5 identifies two critical factors that will determine the winners and losers in this emerging application area. Finally, Section 6 explores strategies for EDI pilot implementation, and Section 7 summarizes our conclusions.

## (2) Definitions: Untangling a New Tower of Babel

As in any new field, every academic researcher, journalist and vendor offers a slightly different definition of systems that are creating electronic linkages between firms. Figure 1 offers a sample of the definitions that have been put forth in recent years and clearly shows the need for a typology to classify different types of IOS. We found few distinctions have been made in regard to the different types of electronic linkages being created between companies. A more careful classification of applications labelled 'interorganizational systems', 'electronic data interchange', and 'electronic markets' is necessary because different applications carry with them different strategic objectives and impacts, as well as unique implementation problems. When we begin to draw conclusions from empirical research, it becomes clear that our findings are not relevant for *all* interorganizational applications of information technology (IT).

For this reason, in Figure 2 we offer a typology of

MIS Quarterly: Interorganizational Information Sharing System is a General Term Referring to Systems that Involve Resources Shared Between Two or More Organizations. (Barret and Konsynski, 1982 ; 94)

Harvard Business Review: Interorganizational Systems (IOS) are Defined as Automated Information Systems Shared by Two or More Companies. These Uses of Information Systems Technology Involve Networks That Transcend Company Boundaries. (Cash and Konsynski, 1985 ; 134)

Fortune: They are Called Channel Systems Because They are Meant to Cure Headaches for People in a Company's Distribution Channels - Commercial Customers and Key Middle Men........In All Cases, by Helping the Customer solve a Problem the Company Supplying the Computer System Stands to Increase Sales or Otherwise Benefit. (Petre, 1985 ; 42)

Link Resources: (Market Research Firm): 'Electronic Data Interchange' is Defined as: Direct Computer-to-Computer Exchange of Standard Business Forms. EDI is Not a System. It is a Standard. . .EDI Consists of a Communications Standard Defining How One Computer is to Talk to Another Computer Over a Network, and a Message Standard Defining the Sequence and Format of Data Which is to be Exchanged. . . . (Quoted in Callahan, 1987 ; 16)

Business Week: In a Nutshell, EDI Allows Specially Formatted Documents, Such as Purchase Orders, to be Sent From One Company's Computer to Another. (1987 ; 80)

Malone, Yates and Benjamin (MIT) : . . .New Information Technologies are Allowing Closer Integration of Adjacent Steps on the Value-Added Chain Through the Development of Electronic Markets and Electronic Hierarchies. (1986 ; 2)

Figure 1. A sample of IOS/EDI definitions

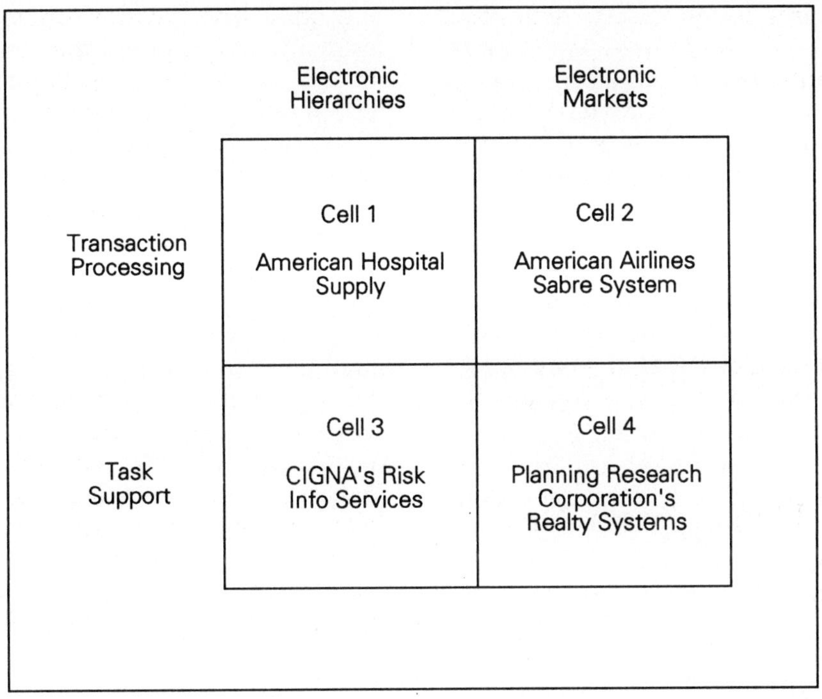

|  | Electronic Hierarchies | Electronic Markets |
|---|---|---|
| Transaction Processing | Cell 1<br><br>American Hospital Supply | Cell 2<br><br>American Airlines Sabre System |
| Task Support | Cell 3<br><br>CIGNA's Risk Info Services | Cell 4<br><br>Planning Research Corporation's Realty Systems |

Figure 2

interorganizational electronic linkages. A review of several dozen systems mentioned in the literature reveals that they do one of two things: (1) routine transaction processing applications, such as order entry or invoicing, or (2) provide non-routine task support for managerial, analytic, and design functions, that contribute to decision making. On the other dimension, these systems are applied either (1) in electronic hierarchies, that is, integrating tasks and functions across a pre-determined set of organizational boundaries; or (2) in electronic markets where multiple buyers and sellers conduct business through an electronic intermediary.

Here are examples of each type of system described in Figure 2:

*Transaction processing/electronic hierarchies* (Cell 1): The classic system in this category is American Hospital Supply, which built what was essentially an electronic order-entry system for its customers. All three of our case studies represent systems of this type, that is, they automate routine transactions between specific buyers and sellers. These are generally the systems that have been categorized as 'electronic data interchange'.

*Transaction processing/electronic markets* (Cell 2): The best known examples of applications in this category are airline reservation systems, such as American Airline's Sabre system. American created an electronic marketplace that allows customers to make routine purchases (reservations) selecting from flights offered by a broad range of airlines.

*Task support/electronic hierarchies* (Cell 3): This class of IOS is distinguished from EDI because these applications provide support for non-routine tasks, such as sales and market analysis, and computer-

aided design. For example, CIGNA Corporation's Risk Information Services enables its corporate customers to access their files on the insurer's computer to do analysis that may help reduce insurance bills. (Petre, 1985:44)

*Task support/electronic markets* (Cell 4): Systems in this category create a marketplace for multiple buyers and sellers, trying to complete non-routine transactions or tasks. For example, Planning Research Corporation's Realty System provides an electronic network that allows real estate agents to search for listings that meet the needs of their customers. The system also provides a range of capabilities which can qualify buyers, calculate closing costs, and analyse sales.

Making distinctions between these four classes of applications is very important, although the boundaries between the four cells are not hard and fast. For the most part, terms describing electronic linkages have been used loosely by academics and practitioners alike, but failure to clarify these concepts will only add to the problems of implementation. In the context of Figure 2, we view 'interorganizational systems', or IOS, as an umbrella term referring to applications in all four cells. We define EDI systems as those transaction processing applications found in Cell 1, although others still use the term more broadly.

Figure 2 is a static view of interorganizational systems, but what is equally important is the evolution of IOS applications over time. Some systems may bridge the categories we have offered, or evolve from one class to another, e.g. electronic hierarchy to market, as previously suggested by Malone, Yates and Benjamin (1986). Another tendency may be to add applications to an IOS so that it provides both transaction processing *and* task support capabilities, in either electronic markets or hierarchies. For example, American Airlines is in the process of introducing a service that will allow companies to automate their travel and entertainment (T & E) information. Building on American's Sabre reservation system, the application automatically transmits booking information to the customer's corporate headquarters with the goal of creating an electronic T & E report for each traveller. (*BusinessWeek*, 9/87:106) This puts American's IOS in both the electronic markets *and* hierarchies cells for transaction processing applications. And, when some customers begin using the new application to analyse T & E costs, the system will also fall into the task support/electronic hierarchy quadrant. This is one example of how EDI systems migrate from cell to cell over time.

Although some of our findings may be relevant to other types of interorganizational systems, the balance of this paper will focus on EDI systems that fall into Cell 1—transaction processing/electronic hierarchies. EDI systems reflect existing patterns of buyer/seller relationships that have been supported by traditional transaction processing systems. Therefore, EDI applications are a natural outgrowth of existing ways of working and they are the most common type of IOS.

## (3) Three Case Studies

The three disguised case studies that provide much of the empirical data for this paper are based on interviews with executives and IS managers in the firms developing the systems. Additional interviews were done with buyers, distributors, and in one case, suppliers using the systems.

### Midwest Tire, Inc. (MTI)*

In the last 5 years, this major tire manufacturer has developed EDI systems with 'original equipment' customers—large automakers—and independent distributors, who sell to the replacement market, as well as suppliers. (See Figure 3) The three types of systems are quite different, however. The original equipment market is highly competitive, given the purchasing power of major auto manufacturers and the unpredictable state of the auto industry in recent years. (The majority of Midwest Tire's sales and profits—85 per cent—come from the replacement market, served primarily by company-owned stores and independent dealers.)

### Customer-directed

Midwest Tire has established electronic linkages with at least five of its original equipment customers, but the specific functions these systems perform vary. For example, General Motors and Ford plants send information about production requirements daily and production schedules weekly to MTI via the EDI system. Midwest Tire, in turn sends ship notices to GM every 2 hours, Monday through Friday, and to Ford hourly between 6:30 am and 11:30 pm on weekdays.

MTI's systems linking it to Navistar and John Deere plants are somewhat different. MTI calls these customers once a day to retrieve daily production schedules. At the same time, it transports ship

---

*All data on Midwest Tire, Inc. in this paper are taken from 'The Impacts of Electronic Integration on Buyers and Suppliers' by Daniel K. Callahan, 1987.

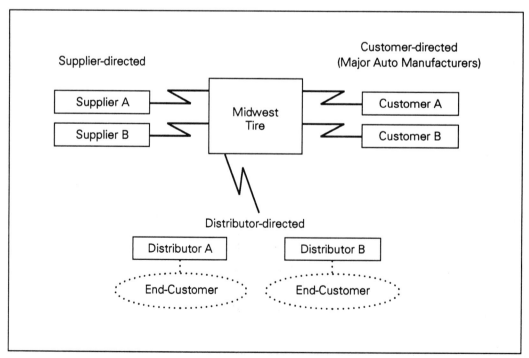

Figure 3. Midwest Tire, Inc. three forms of EDI

notices for orders sent out that day. Caterpillar also sends daily production requirements to Midwest Tire on a different network. In early 1987, at least three other auto manufacturers were in the process of implementing systems with MTI that would allow daily exchange of production information and advance ship notices.

Orders for original equipment tires currently come to MTI by computer, telephone, and teletype. Those received by computer links now represent about 50 per cent of the dollar volume in original equipment sales. These EDI systems have increased information provided to Midwest Tire's product coordinators and, thus, have streamlined the process of matching customer orders with MTI's production.

### Distributor-directed

In addition to a system that links Midwest Tire's company-owned stores to the firm's inventory management system, MTI has also developed an EDI application tying it to independent tire distributors. This system, still in the pilot stage at the time of the study, allows distributors to do on-line order entry, order status inquiry, and product availability checks. The major part of the transaction process that has been changed by this electronic link is the medium used to transmit orders. The computer instead of the telephone can now be used to communicate routine orders.

### Supplier-directed

In the supply chain, Midwest Tire has electronic links with at least four companies. As with the systems in the customer chain, each one works differently and fulfills slightly different functions. MTI has a direct link to a major battery supplier in the large replacement market. Midwest Tire stocks

batteries in its company-owned stores and is one of the manufacturer's largest customers. With the system, MTI calls the manufacturer once a day and transmits its orders. At the same time, it picks up the supplier's 'confirming orders'.

Each day Midwest Tire places orders electronically with other suppliers who manufacture shock absorbers and brake shoes. Unlike the link with the battery supplier, communication with these suppliers is unidirectional from MTI. In another case, a motor freight company dials up a remote printer connected to Midwest Tire's network and once a day downloads freight bills of loading information.

### Office Technologies Corporation (OTC)*

Office Technologies Corporation manufactures a broad line of business equipment and office supplies. The firm has a large share of the office copier market. The OTC case study examined four EDI systems in the Customer Services Organization of the firm's U.S. Marketing Group. Five Customer Administration Centres in this unit are responsible for all after-sale administrative tasks. The centres process order entry, billing, and credit transactions. In the long run, the EDI systems described below are intended to replace the clerical components of these functions. In addition, unlike the other cases we studied, those EDI applications are all designed to become part of a broad range of services that ultimately will enhance customer support. (See Figure 4).

(1) An electronic ordering system allows customers to order a variety of OTC products and supplies. With this system the customer sends a

---

*All data on Office Technologies Corporation in this paper are taken from 'Impact of Electronic Linkages between a Firm and Its Customers' by Shyamal Choudhury, 1987.

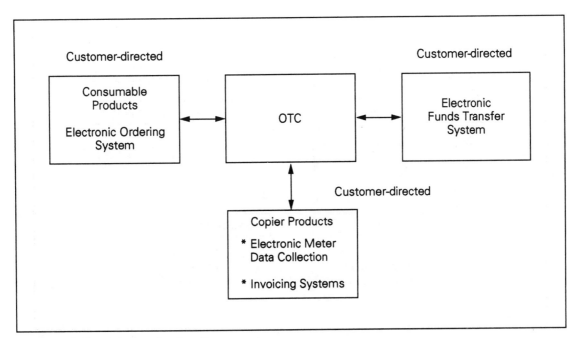

Figure 4. EDI at Office Technologies Corporation

purchase order electronically to OTC and receives immediate confirmation that the order has been received. In addition, a purchase order acknowledgement is sent to the customer electronically after the contents of the order have been verified. Currently, OTC's receiving hardware in this electronic link is not integrated with its computerized order entry system, so orders received on a PC must be printed out and rekeyed. Four technical configurations are currently being supported by OTC because of differing hardware at the customer's end.

(2) An electronic meter data collection system facilitates the copier billing process for OTC. Each month customers must read the meters showing the number of copies made on their machines leased from OTC. Previously, these meter reads were mailed to OTC by customers on pre-printed meter cards, so that bills could be prepared. However, about 50 per cent of these hand-processed cards were not mailed or were in error, which required time consuming follow-up phone calls for OTC. But with the new system the customer collects the meter reads and transmits them electronically to an OTC computer. This eliminates the filling out and handling of meter cards. In addition, with the electronic system, receipt of the data can be confirmed and validated when it is input, thus, eliminating the error correction cycle.

(3) An electronic invoicing system sends invoices from an OTC computer to a customer computer. This eliminates the need to mail printed invoices, as well as the need for customers to rekey invoices. The biggest advantage of this system is that OTC knows when an invoice has entered into the customer's computer system and therefore can forecast cash flow more precisely. Currently, however, OTC's billing system extracts a translation of the invoice and puts it on a computer tape which is mailed to the customer for direct loading onto their computer. Direct computer-to-computer upgrades will be introduced soon. Three customers are currently using this electronic invoicing system.

(4) With the electronic funds transfer system, instead of mailing a check, the customer releases payment through a computer-to-computer communication link between the customer and its bank. The bank then debits the customer account and can credit OTC immediately if their account is in the same bank. If the accounts are in different banks, the electronic funds transfer is done using the National Automated Clearing House Agency format which is an established standard. OTC has been receiving electronic payments this way for 2 years from several large banks and a major oil company, and it is currently involved in a pilot system with a division of General Motors.

*Western Food Company**
Western Food Company is one of the largest manufacturers of food and beverages in the United States. It offers a broad range of products and has significant marketshare in many categories, including coffee, powdered soft drinks, breakfast cereals, frozen vegetables, and dessert lines. The primary user of EDI systems at Western is the Distribution and Sales Service Division (DSSD). This division is responsible for delivering Western's 'dry' grocery products from its warehouses to the warehouses and stores of its customers. DSSD's 15 distribution centres around the country must handle the purchase order, invoice processing, and customer service for every independent and chain-owned grocery store in the U.S. The primary mission of the distribution centres is to minimize the handling, storage, transportation, and processing costs that must be charged back to the product divisions, while at the same time providing excellent service to customers.

Western is currently using EDI systems based on a Uniform Communications Standard (UCS) with 21 of its wholesale distributor customers. The systems generally are used by wholesalers to transmit purchase orders and to receive invoices, as well as purchase order acceptance/rejection messages from Western.

The major change created by Western's EDI system is that its distribution centres no longer need to be directly involved in the flow of purchase order and invoicing information. (See Figure 5) With the electronic link, POs are transmitted directly from the customer's computer to a mini-computer front-end at Western's headquarters, bypassing completely the distribution centres which traditionally collected POs and entered them into the firm's order processing system. A similar process is followed with invoices, which, in the ideal situation with EDI, are transmitted directly from Western's HQ into the distributor's accounts payable system. At this stage, however, most distributors still print out the electronic invoices before entering them into internal systems or processing them manually.

*Summary of Three Cases*
Perhaps because all three cases represent EDI applications in mature industries or product areas, there are many more similarities than differences in these systems. All three companies have attempted to automate the product ordering process in businesses where keeping costs low and providing excellent service are both critical success factors. These systems are also not affected by fast changing product lines or unstable markets. The products they are selling are for the most part high volume, relatively simple products. In keeping with these

---

*All data on Western Food Company in this paper are taken from 'Electronic Integration between Firms: A Case Study in the Grocery Industry' by J. Thomas Gormley III, 1987.

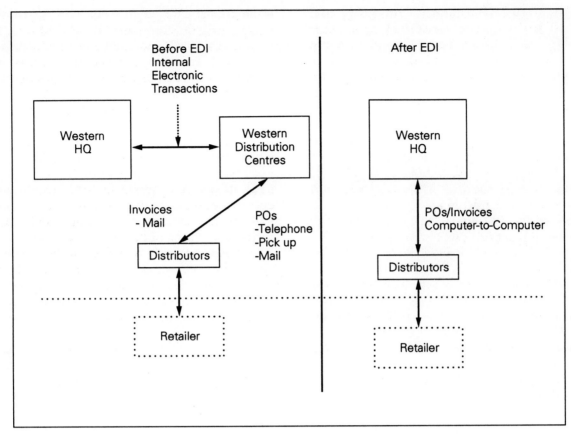

Figure 5. EDI at Western Food Company

product characteristics, the systems are inevitably linked to long-term buyers who have relatively stable relationships with the supplier. The buyers, for the initial systems anyway, are all high volume customers.

In all three companies the systems are overwhelmingly buyer or distributor-oriented, which conforms to the overall trend of IOS reported on in the literature to date. In our sample, the only backward-integrated, or supplier-oriented, system studied was at Midwest Tire.

The three cases present systems in varying degrees of maturity and sophistication. Midwest Tire's electronic links to GM and Ford are well established, while Office Technology's electronic invoicing system is still in the pilot stages. Overall, the systems studied are relatively new, the standards and related technology are still evolving, and the penetration of the systems is limited. For example, at Midwest Tire, 50 per cent of sales orders received from auto manufacturers come via the computer. The remainder still come by telephone and teletype. At Western Food Company, 20 per cent of the firm's total customer transactions are handled by an electronic network. These represent some of the more mature EDI systems.

The EDI applications in these cases are performing simple, inelegant tasks and they are not integrated, for the most part, with the firm's internal systems. For example, in Office Technology's electronic ordering system there is, as yet, no electronic link between the hardware receiving purchase orders and OTC's computerized order entry system. Orders received through EDI must be rekeyed into the firm's internal system. This rekeying appears to be a relatively common practice for new EDI applications.

Finally, as we will see in the next section, the technology used for EDI is still very unsettled and standards remain a major factor in the spread of this type of IOS.

## (4) Impacts of EDI—Competitive Advantage or Necessity?

Gaining competitive advantage from EDI applications is much more difficult than it might appear. The academic and business press has focused overwhelmingly on the relatively few success stories to be found in firms implementing interorganizational systems. Like lottery winners, however, these cases create unrealistic hopes for the rest of us. Although the odds are a little better than the lottery, the prospects of hitting the jackpot with an EDI application are still slim.

The desire for strategic advantage remains the most commonly espoused reason for implementing EDI systems. But of the eight different applications in the three companies studied, only one system—MTI's distributor-oriented system—showed the potential of providing significant competitive advantage by gaining first-mover benefits that included potentially locking out other suppliers with proprietary technology. While the other seven had the potential of reducing costs, in industries where the low cost position is important to success, the savings would not be enough to provide strategic benefits.

In reality, at least six of the EDI systems in this sample were motivated by competitive necessity. Management on the supplier's side believed the systems *had* to be developed as a defensive measure to stay even with the competition, although there was no evidence that the three firms were being hurt by competitor's systems. Since the two parties to EDI transactions are buyer and supplier, let us examine the impacts on each.

*Impacts on Suppliers*

One of the most striking aspects of the eight different systems in our sample was how little change they had created in the supplier's organization. Staff reductions have been few, if any, as all three companies tried to avoid laying off workers when the systems were first installed. Instead of reducing headcount, the tendency has been to try to increase the productivity of those using the systems. Implicit in this approach is a minimal change in work processes. Gormley's study of Western Food Company provides a typical example. He reports:

> Little organizational change has occurred in either Western or its customers. Each has maintained the same number of order entry personnel on its staff. None of the customer service coordinators or clerical workers have been elevated in salary or title as a result of their experience with [EDI], and the learning of new skills. It appears that such organizational change would be viewed negatively by managers and subordinates. (Gormley, 1987:153)

Along with few staff reductions, there was very little change in the tasks performed by those using the systems. One exception to this is the system linking Midwest Tire to its independent distributors. This order entry application has changed the skills needed by customer service representatives. Because orders are now placed electronically, instead of by telephone, there is less need for good telephone skills and product familiarity, and more focus on reviewing information entered by customers on the computer.

The relatively minor changes created by these EDI systems to date have resulted in only small cost savings for Midwest Tire, Office Technologies, and Western. Cost savings for suppliers will continue to be minimal as long as the penetration of EDI remains small and it is necessary to maintain parallel non-EDI systems.

In general, the short term benefits of EDI for suppliers tend to be intangible. In all three cases, the systems improved the firm's service-oriented image and enhanced its role as an industry leader in the application of technology. Because all three companies are selling in mature markets, automating its

transactions gives the seller a way of at least temporarily differentiating itself from the competition, by handling sales transactions more efficiently. This advantage, however, is short-lived as other suppliers instal similar electronic capabilities. In one instance, for example, Midwest Tire found that its EDI system with a truck manufacturer gave it a 6 to 9 month advantage over other tire suppliers, until they established a similar electronic link with the customer.

In all three cases, suppliers built EDI systems out of competitive necessity, and there was *no* measurable gain in business volume attributable to the applications. For the supplier, EDI systems often turn out to be a cost of doing business and a way of learning about the technology. In addition, however, they also may lead to other more sophisticated forms of IOS, such as Midwest Tire's subsequent electronic collaboration with an auto manufacturer on new tread design. This is an example of an IOS application involving task support in an electronic hierarchy, as illustrated by Cell 3 in Figure 2.

In summary, the only way suppliers will be able to continually differentiate themselves from competitors implementing EDI systems is by adding new capabilities.

*Impact on Buyers*

Buyers, on the other hand, tend to gain more immediate and measurable benefits—cost savings—from EDI applications. These come, not because the customer has done anything innovative, but simply because of their structural position in the marketplace. Cost savings come from the buyer's ability to use more timely product ordering and shipment information to reduce inventory, as well as improving materials management and productivity. For example, when Midwest Tire established an EDI with some of its parts suppliers, the time between placing an order and delivery dropped about 6 days. This created an estimated one-time inventory reduction of $250,000 and an added savings of $250,000 in inventory carrying costs. In addition, better information about the status and location of products that had been ordered, e.g., when a shipment would arrive, improved warehouse planning and personnel scheduling. Being able to schedule unloading more accurately meant less need for overtime labour and generally improved warehouse productivity.

As with suppliers, the effect of EDI on buyers' headcount appears more limited than might be expected. A recent study of EDI use by purchasing departments, however, found that organizations with the most mature systems reported reductions in personnel, while those EDI projects in the pilot or planning stages reported no decline in headcount. 'This seems to indicate that reductions in personnel are not expected but may result,' concludes Emmelhainz. (1986:7)

One unanticipated benefit of EDI for buyers is improved information about suppliers' operations. This can provide a significant advantage when negotiating with the supplier. For example, Callahan observed, 'Midwest Tire's customer-directed systems show that, contrary to earlier "wisdom" regarding interorganizational systems, these systems do *not* result in increased power of suppliers relative to buyers. Midwest Tire's customers, in fact now have more control over the company in that they have shipment information broken out by plant, size, product line and dollar-volume equivalent.' (Callahan, 1987:88)

## (5) Critical Factors in EDI Development

Our research indicates that two factors more than any others influence an organization's ability to develop effective EDI applications. These are (1) the existence of industry standards, and (2) the firm's ability to manage necessary changes in organizational structure and work processes.

### Standards

The state of standards development is a critical variable in the evolution of EDI within individual firms and across industries. The existence of standards is not only a prerequisite for the high volume penetration of EDI which can lead to significant cost savings, but standards also change the competitive dynamics of these interorganizational systems because they change the rules of success. The evolution of widely-accepted EDI standards within an industry lowers the cost of entering into electronic linkages with buyers and suppliers. This makes proprietary systems, such as those developed by early EDI 'winners' like American Hospital Supply and McKesson, impractical or at least much more difficult to 'sell' to trading partners. In addition, standards solidify a new, larger market for vendors and encourage them to create better EDI software tools and third party networks.

Progress in standards development varies greatly from industry to industry. The evolution of standards seems to depend a great deal on industry structure, the strategies of early EDI adopters within an industry, the spirit of cooperation that exists between firms, and the strength of industry associations. Industries with strong trade associations, e.g. transportation, groceries, or where regulatory standards are imposed, e.g., banking, airlines, are most likely to be early developers of EDI standards.

Dominant buyers in manufacturing industries, such as autos, are also likely to be interested in EDI systems because of the technology's ability to support 'just-in-time' inventory control. These buyers can initially impose their own standards on suppliers, but their interest in expanding penetration of the technology more quickly may lead the buyer to become a force behind standards development, as happened in the auto industry.

In industries where standards do not exist or have not yet evolved sufficiently, each EDI link requires significantly more effort on the part of buyer and seller. Midwest Tire, for example, incurred substantial development costs in creating customized document interfaces for EDI systems linking MTI to its major customers. These systems, implemented at the request of the auto manufacturers, had to be designed to suit the unique specifications of each buyer because industry standards had not yet been developed. In this case, as in others in our sample, the party that conforms when standards do not exist is usually the seller.

Because standards have yet to evolve in most industries, the value-added networks (VANs), such as GEISCO and Tymnet, offer firms translation capabilities that make it easier for companies to translate their internal transactions into acceptable interorganizational standards, such as ANSI X.12, a document-messaging format standard developed by the American National Standards Institute. These third party networks not only reduce the cost of code and protocol conversions, they also offer an established distribution system, or network, with low incremental costs for linking up to additional firms.

Of course, not all companies are anxious to establish EDI standards. For example, when suppliers see an opportunity for 'significant' competitive advantage, it is in their interest to preempt any evolving standards and create their own proprietary protocols. An example from our sample is Midwest Tire's attempt to create an order entry system for independent distributors using proprietary hardware and software in order to create switching costs, while enhancing service, for its customers.

The existence of standards both within a particular industry and across industries has important implications for the potential strategic impacts of EDI systems. As the development of intra-industry EDI standards gains momentum, customized systems such as the one at Midwest Tire above will become increasingly hard to 'sell' to trading partners. In addition, the data show that over the long term the balance of power will continue to shift to buyers. Well-defined standards not only eliminate barriers to entry and encourage more suppliers to install EDI systems but they also remove switching costs for buyers and give them more leverage over suppliers.

### Managing Change in Structure and Work Design

Ultimately, the critical factor in determining which firms derive the greatest benefits from EDI will be the ability to manage major changes in work design and organizational structure. The notion that in the long term significant internal restructuring will be necessary to reap the potential benefits of EDI was lurking in the background of all three cases. We found, however, a paradox in the EDI projects we studied and the 15 reported on by Emmelhainz.

As part of their strategy to gain organizational acceptance of the systems, developers in all three firms intentionally minimized any changes in the work processes affected by these systems. This virtually eliminated resistance to the project within the organization, but it also meant the benefits, and specifically cost savings, derived from the systems were minimal, thus, making it more difficult to justify expansion. Of the companies studied, only developers at Office Technologies explicitly recognized the need to redesign work processes as EDI transaction volume builds up.

Organizations implementing EDI systems are faced with a dilemma. Staying in the pilot mode of operation minimizes painful organizational change but also results in increased costs of using the technology without deriving significant savings. The alternative is to go through a disruptive and uncomfortable redesign of work processes to take full advantage of EDI technology, which inherently requires fewer people doing different tasks.

Although there is no hard evidence at this stage for any of the cases investigated, it seems apparent that when EDI begins to dominate the volume of transactions, organizations will have to redesign business processes in order to remain cost and service competitive. What is less clear, however, is whether the transition to new organizational processes and structure can be facilitated in the earlier pilot stages of implementation.

## (6) Strategies for Pilot Implementation

Most companies get started with EDI technology through pilot projects. The exceptions are those firms driven by dominant buyers to establish electronic linkages.

Pilots are essentially processes designed to facilitate organizational learning. It is only logical that any firm entering this applications area for the first time will do a series of pilot projects before trying to put a system into production. Indeed, the three companies in this study did extensive pilot projects to learn about the technological and organizational impacts of the systems. Ironically, in the early stages of EDI development, considerations about competitive advantage are rarely a concern. The focus is on making the technology work and managing the impacts of the application on the organization. Office Technologies, for example, ran pilots for each of its four types of EDI applications primarily to determine any obstacles to implementation, not

to collect data on the pros and cons of installing such systems.

EDI pilots tend to be technologically simple. They minimize changes to existing data processing transaction systems and they can be implemented without sophisticated technology. At Office Technologies, early EDI prototypes simply involved receiving data on two PCs in ANSI X.12 format. Developers intentionally avoided more complicated technical hookups, such as interfacing the PCs with a mainframe, which could provide remote order entry or inventory checking in OTC's data bases. Except for some standards translation software, EDI developers in our sample tended to use well-established technologies and communication networks.

Another important factor in EDI pilot implementation is senior management support for the project. Except in cases where EDI is forced on a company by outside pressures, top management must understand that the implementation process takes time and is a long term competitive necessity. They must also recognize that, ultimately, to secure substantial benefits from EDI will require organizational redesign.

One of the functions of the pilot should be to provide senior management sponsors with the necessary learning and insights about the above factors to help them plan and support future EDI expansion. As a rule, however, executives seem to abdicate any control over where EDI prototypes are developed in the firm, nor do they review the strategic implications of these applications. In our case studies, the link between senior management and the EDI project, while strong at the outset, disappeared soon after the pilots were developed.

Important questions remain about the proper role for top management in shaping the organization's policy toward interorganizational systems and the allocation of resources for these systems. For example, should decisions about specific EDI applications be made far down in the organization, or should they be dictated from the top? Should the political motivations of various units in the firm who stand to gain from EDI be ignored? There is little doubt about the importance of top management's role in formulating an IOS strategy, but the level of involvement in EDI development remains an unanswered question.

Despite optimistic assumptions about the ability of developers to expand EDI use beyond the prototype stage, significantly increasing the penetration of these systems often proves more difficult than expected. Moving EDI systems into production means confronting not only barriers imposed by a lack of standards, but also the organization's resistance to large-scale change. Top management support in this process is essential because experience indicates that the ability to implement a successful EDI pilot, while essential for learning, is no guarantee that the application can be readily expanded to a broader group of users.

# (7) Conclusion

Until now, electronic data interchange has been viewed largely as a strategic issue whose major implementation challenge is overcoming the technical problems of creating electronic links between firms. This, however, is an oversimplification of what the technology means to organizations and what must be done to use it effectively.

As we stated at the outset, EDI represents a specific class of interorganizational systems, and the concept carries with it a unique set of strategic and implementation considerations. Contrary to popular assumptions, the majority of EDI applications will be built out of competitive necessity, providing little, if any, competitive advantage for most users. These systems will become a cost of doing business.

To be sure, many firms enjoy a competitive advantage from EDI, however short lived. But only a rare few maintain this advantage, and when they do it is *not* from the technology but by instilling a mindset that focuses on customer value and then supports a process that continually innovates and adds features valuable to the customer.

The existence of standards will continue to be the fundamental factor in how fast EDI spreads in an industry. In the end, two determinants of this spread will be (1) industries with strong trade associations which create standards, and (2) industries where a few major buyers are able to force suppliers to establish electronic linkages. As standards become more widespread over time, more of the benefits of EDI will go to buyers, who will find these systems shifting the strategic balance of power in their favour. Thus, buyers will be the dominant force behind the growth of EDI, while suppliers will push it only when they see some way of differentiating themselves.

The most significant and, heretofore, most overlooked factor in determining the effective use of EDI is the organization's ability to manage the changes in structure and work processes that must attend the implementation of this technology. Laying EDI systems on top of existing work processes trivializes the potential of these interorganizational systems. To assure effective use of the technology, organizational redesign must become synonymous with EDI development. The managers who understand this will will be most likely to succeed in an environment where EDI becomes a way of doing business.

Those who do gain significant competitive advantage from EDI will do so by learning how to integrate the technology effectively into their organizations in such a way that they can continually add valuable new capabilities to the system, while deriving cost savings from increased productivity and decreased overhead made possible by EDI. In the early stages, most of this learning will come by implementing pilot projects, but competing with EDI is not simply a matter of investing in the technology. EDI development is a process that takes time and patience, and those who start first have the best chance of staying ahead of the competition if they recognize that EDI involves a continuous process of change. There is no end to organizational change in this era of rapidly evolving information technology.

*References*

(1) Stephanie Barrett and Benn R. Konsynski, Inter-organization information sharing systems, *MIS Quarterly*, pp. 93–105, December (1982).

(2) Robert I. Benjamin and Michael S. Scott Morton, Information technology, integration, and organizational change, Center for Information Systems Research, Working Paper No. 138, also Management in the 1990s Working Paper 86-017, Sloan School of Management, MIT, Cambridge, April (1986).

(3) Business is turning data into a potent strategic weapon, *BusinessWeek*, pp. 92–98, 22 August (1983).

(4) Daniel K. Callahan, The impacts of electronic integration on buyers and suppliers. Master's Thesis, Sloan School of Management, MIT, Cambridge, Mass., May (1987).

(5) James I. Cash Jr and Benn R. Konsynski, IS redraws competitive boundaries, *Harvard Business Review*, pp. 134–142, March/April (1985).

(6) Shyamal Choudhury, Impact of electronic linkages between a firm and its customer. Master's Thesis, Sloan School of Management, MIT, Cambridge, Mass., June (1987).

(7) An electronic pipeline that's changing the way America does business, *BusinessWeek*, pp. 80–81, 3 August (1987).

(8) Margaret Anne Emmelhainz, Executive summary: the impact of EDI on the purchasing process. Unpublished report, October (1986).

(9) Margaret Anne Emmelhainz, The impact of electronic data interchange on the purchasing process. (2 vols.) Working Paper 87-3, The Center for Business and Economic Research, School of Business Administration, University of Dayton, Dayton, Ohio, February (1987).

(10) J. Thomas Gormley III, Electronic integration between firms: a case study in the grocery industry. Master's Thesis, Sloan School of Management, MIT, Cambridge, Mass., May (1987).

(11) Blake Ives and Gerard P. Learmonth, The information system as a competitive weapon, *Communications of the ACM*, **27** (12), 1193–1201, December (1984).

(12) Patricia Keefe, Can you afford to ignore EDI? *Computerworld* Focus, pp. 39–42, 6 January (1988).

(13) Thomas W. Malone, JoAnne Yates and Robert I. Benjamin, Electronic markets and electronic hierarchies, Center for Information Systems Research, Working Paper No. 137, also Management in the 1990s Working Paper 86-018, Sloan School of Management, MIT, Cambridge, Mass., April (1986).

(14) Barbara Canning McNurlin, The rise of 'cooperative' systems, *EDP Analyzer*, **25** (6), 1–16, June (1987).

(15) M. H. Notowidigdo, Information systems: weapons to gain the competitive edge, *Financial Executive,* **LII** (2), 20–25, February (1984).

(16) Now, the 'paperless' expense account, *BusinessWeek,* p. 106, 7 September (1987).

(17) Otis MIS: going up, *InformationWEEK,* pp. 32–37, 18 May (1987).

(18) Peter Petre, How to keep customers happy captives, *Fortune,* pp. 42–46, 2 September (1985).

(19) Michael E. Porter and Victor E. Millar, How information gives you competitive advantage, *Harvard Business Review,* pp. 149–160, July/August (1985).

(20) David G. Robinson and Steve A. Stanton, Exploit EDI before EDI exploits you, *Journal of information strategy,* pp. 32–35, Spring (1987).

(21) Brunce Rubinger, Technology policy in Japanese firms: decision-making, supplier links, and technical goals, in Mel Horwitch (Ed.), *Technology in the Modern Corporation: A Strategic Perspective,* Pergamon Press, Elmsford, New York (1986).

(22) Paul E. Schindler Jr, Subject: McKesson casebook study, *The Magazine for the Information Age,* **1.3,** Fall (1987).

(23) Patricia Taylor, EDI setting standard for future, *Computerworld,* p. 117, 14 December (1987).

(24) Tishman builds on MIS cornerstone, *InformationWEEK,* pp. 27–28, 10 August (1987).

(25) Charles Wiseman and Ian C. MacMillan, Creating competitive weapons from information systems, *Journal of Business Strategy,* **5** (4), 42–49, Fall (1984).